# Disciples

Year 2

# living in community

## Carol M. Bechtel

FAITH
ALIVE®
Christian Resources

Grand Rapids, Michigan

This study is part of *Disciples,* year 2, a comprehensive multiyear faith formation program for adults. Year 2 studies build on the foundation laid by the studies in year 1.

Year 2 includes the following study guides, which feature daily readings for each session:

- Prayer
- Reading the Bible
- Worship
- Living in Community
- Overcoming Sin

# Contents

# Introduction

A song that was popular on *Sesame Street* years ago went like this:

One banana, two bananas—
one for me and one for you bananas.
You'll never see one alone on a tree,
'cause bananas don't grow alone (no, no, no).
Bananas don't grow alone!

As my kids and I sang along with Big Bird one afternoon, it occurred to me that what's true of bananas is true of Christians as well. *We* don't grow very well alone either.

This is not to say that individual growth in faith is not important. At baptism every believer embarks on a path that will lead us, like Jesus, to increase "in wisdom and in favor with God and people" (Luke 2:52). In the Reformed family of faith, the word for this path is *sanctification*.

Yet we often forget that this process of individual growth happens *in the context of Christian community*. Christians—like

> **Word Alert**
>
> We use the word *sanctification* to describe the lifelong process of growth that follows our redemption in Christ. This process fills us "with the knowledge of [God's] will through all the wisdom and understanding that the Spirit gives, so that [we] may live a life worthy of the Lord . . . bearing fruit in every good work, growing in the knowledge of God, . . . filled with the knowledge of God's will" (Col. 1:9b-10).

bananas—don't grow alone. We are called into a community of fellow disciples that helps to shape and nourish us. This community, in turn, exists to worship and serve God *together*.

The focus of this study is on the crucial place of community in the life of Christian disciples. It addresses questions such as these:

- What are the behaviors, practices, problems, and rewards of Christian community?

- How does Christian community cut against the grain of our individualistic culture?

- Why is community so essential for Christian discipleship? That is, what is there about being a Christian that means we cannot, by definition, "go it alone"?

## About This Book

There are five sections in this study. The first one is "Foundations." It attempts to lay the groundwork for Christian community from biblical texts in the Old and New Testaments. The next three sections are devoted to different facets of our life together in Christian community: worship[1], fellowship, and challenges. The study concludes with a section on witness, our task as a Christian community.

Those of you who are veterans of *Disciples* (Year 2) are already familiar with its format. But you may not have thought about how this format combines the individual and the community in much the same way as that bunch of bananas does.

---

[1] Another whole study in this series is devoted to worship. Consider this section a "preview of coming attractions." Here we will focus on those aspects of worship that are most specifically related to Christian life in community.

Each week has five daily readings, followed by material meant to guide a small group (community!) discussion of the week's theme. Taking time to read the daily readings day by day, thinking about them through the week, and sharing them with others will deepen your understanding and help you to experience for yourself that Christians grow best in "bunches."

You may use the daily readings for your own personal devotions, or you may read them with others (in the family, a prayer group, roommates, or others). Even if you are reading them on your own, remember that the others in your group are reading them as well. This will give you a sense of being together even when you are apart.

Please take the time to read the Bible references that begin each daily reading as well as any others that are scattered through the study. Look them up, ponder them, read them aloud, and read the verses around them. This will both enrich your devotional time and help to connect you with that great "cloud of witnesses" (Heb 12:1)—the Christian community throughout the ages, the communion of saints.

# Session 1
# Foundations

# Created for Community 1

*"The Lord God said, 'It is not good for the man to be alone. I will make a helper suitable for him.'"*

—Genesis 2:18

Gardeners and farmers will immediately appreciate the wisdom of God's words in Genesis 2:18. It *isn't* good to be alone when there's a world of work to be done. This reality is almost certainly the genesis of the proverb "Many hands make light work."

Growing up on a farm gave me many opportunities to experience this firsthand. Certain jobs were simply impossible to do alone, especially with old-fashioned farming equipment (unlike some of today's machines that do everything but button up your overalls!). Take haying, for instance. The heat was often oppressive, and the chaff working its way down the back of a sweaty shirt was enough to make you want to run screaming for the shower. If the weather threatened rain, there was an added sense of urgency. But at the end of the day, when the bales were stacked in the barn and we sat in the shade enjoying ginger ale and pie, we shared a deep sense of satisfaction . . . not to mention the laughter that somehow seemed to trump our tired muscles. It was one of those communal moments when the whole really was greater than the sum of its parts.

Of course, in the passage above, God must have had more in mind than Adam's workload. The issue of procreation must have been a factor as well! Interestingly, though, Genesis 2 puts less emphasis on the command to "be fruitful and multiply" than does Genesis 1 (see Gen 1:22, 28). Genesis 2 gives us the sense that *companionship* is important as well. After noting Adam's lonely state, God first parades the animals and birds in front of Adam, but alas, "for Adam no suitable helper was found" (v. 20). Only Eve—the woman sculpted from Adam's side—will do. It's an appropriate symbol of the equality and mutuality of the first human relationship. In fact, Adam and Eve are "made for each other."

While the subject of this study is specifically *Christian* community, it makes sense to begin by acknowledging that God has created *all* human beings for community. Whether we realize it or not, community

> **Word Alert**
>
> Behind the English word *helper* lies the Hebrew word, *'ezer*. Unlike the English word, however, the Hebrew has no connotations of inferiority. It is used to describe God in several psalms (see 10:14; 30:10; 54:4).

is written into our DNA by the author of creation. We were never intended to be "rugged individualists" who move through life without needing other people—the kind of people immortalized in James Bond "007" movies.

A careful reading of the Bible suggests that this communal aspect of our nature is rooted in the very character of God. Genesis 1:27 asserts that human beings—both male and female—are created in God's image. In the early church, believers articulated the communal character of God by talking about the Trinity. As God exists in relationship (Father, Son, and Holy Spirit), so human beings created in God's image exist in relationship (with each other, the rest of creation, and with our Creator).

If community is so much a part of who we are as humans, why do we try so hard to "go it alone"? The answer may have something to do with what our culture values.

In his book *Simply Christian: Why Christianity Makes Sense*, N. T. Wright talks about how children growing up in an African village experience a vast extended family:

> . . . Every adult within walking distance [is] treated as an honorary aunt or uncle in a way that is unimaginable in the modern West. In such a community, there exist multiple networks of support, encouragement, rebuke, and warning. . . . [By contrast,] those who live in today's Western world mostly don't even realize what they're missing. In fact, they might be alarmed at the thought of all that togetherness.

As the mother of teens, I am less alarmed than jealous when I read about such an extended family. I may not know exactly what I'm missing, but I can glimpse it when I read Wright's description and when I reflect on Genesis 1-2.

How about you? What do these reflections on our basic communal character make you long for in your own life and in our life together?

## Think It Over

1.  What aspects of modern life work against community? What makes community hard for you? Do you think of yourself as a "rugged individualist?

2.  What is your most powerful memory/experience of community?

## In Other Words

"Two are better than one. . . . If they fall down, they can help each other up. But pity those who fall and have no one to help them up! Also, if two lie down together, they will keep warm. But how can one keep warm alone? Though one may be overpowered, two can defend themselves. A cord of three strands is not quickly broken."

—Ecclesiastes 4:9-12

## Live It Out

Turn off your TV for an evening and attend a community event— a city council meeting, a basketball game, or volunteer for a few hours at a local cause.

# Blessed to Be a Blessing 2

> *"I will make you into a great nation, and I will bless you; I will make your name great, and you will be a blessing. I will bless those who bless you, and whoever curses you I will curse; and all peoples on earth will be blessed through you."*
>
> —Genesis 12:2-3

It may seem strange to begin our study on Christian community looking at texts from the Old Testament. And yet, what we call the Old Testament was the "Bible" Jesus knew. He must have gone to Hebrew school with his friends and learned the language of that Scripture.

So what would Jesus have learned from this pivotal passage in Genesis 12, commonly referred to as "the call of Abraham"? Let's follow in Jesus' footsteps for a moment and read with an eye for what this story teaches about both God and the community of faith.

Abram (a.k.a. Abraham) must have felt pretty special when God showed up with this announcement in Genesis 12: "I will bless you; I will make your name great." Who wouldn't be flattered, after all, if the Lord of the universe showed up with the news that you'd soon be rich and famous?

But God barely gives Abraham's head time to swell before making it clear that this is not just "about him." Abraham, God is quick to explain, is about to become a great means to an even greater end. He is blessed *so that all peoples on earth will be blessed*.

So what do we learn about God here? First, it's clear that God has an agenda. Second, that agenda is so sweeping that it impacts all of creation. It's easy to lose sight of this since so much of the passage is focused on Abraham and his obedient response to God's call. But the bottom line is this: Abraham and his descendents have been singled out by God to play a part in a much larger mission—a mission of grace and redemption that has implications for the whole world. And this leads us to another observation about God; that God often shows compassion by using *the few* to bless *the many*.

And what do we learn about Abraham? To answer this we really need to "read around" verses 2-3. Verse 1 makes the cost of the call specific: God commands Abraham, "Go from your country, your people and your father's household to the land I will show you." It's interesting that God doesn't give any reasons for choosing Abraham. The quality of Abraham's character is clear from his response to the call: "So Abraham went, as the LORD had told him" (v. 4). And this at the ripe old age of 75!

It is surely an honor when an individual or a community of faith is called by God to be an instrument of God's grace in the world. But that call does not come without a cost, and obedience can demand "our soul, our life, our all."

That last quote is from the hymn "When I Survey the Wondrous Cross" by Isaac Watts, a hymn that focuses our attention on the One who showed us the true meaning of obedience: Jesus Christ. He became "obedient to death—even death on a cross!" (Phil 2:8).

Did Jesus think of Abraham's "costly call" even as he demonstrated the last full measure of his own obedience on the cross? We can't be sure, of course. But we can surely suspect that he was hearing the other great echo reverberating between the cross and that call of Abraham, namely, God's determination to use *one* to bless *many*. Jesus' willingness to go to the cross demonstrates the lengths to which God was willing to go to accomplish that ancient, sweeping agenda.

The story of Dietrich Bonhoeffer is another illustration of God's agenda and the cost of obedience. Bonheoffer is remembered for his determined and costly witness for Christ in Nazi Germany. Though friends begged him to flee to safety, Bonhoeffer remained with his "flock," teaching at a clandestine seminary in Finkenwalde, Germany, in defiance of both the state church and the Nazi regime. There he wrote a classic book about faith in community, *Life Together*, as well as *The Cost of Discipleship*.

The cost of Bonhoeffer's own discipleship soon became clear. In April of 1943, Bonhoeffer was arrested. He spent time in Gestapo prisons in Berlin, Buchenwald, Schönberg, and finally, Flossenberg. On April 8, 1945—just weeks before the end of the war—Bonhoeffer was hanged by the Nazis.

If we think about Bonhoeffer's story on the level of the *one*, it is a tragedy. But if we think about it in terms of the *many,* it is a triumph. His witness has blessed generations of Christians, not only through the writings that were forged in the furnace of that terrible time, but in the impact he had on the people around him in prison. They were, we are told, from "all the families of the earth."

I wonder if Bonhoeffer and Abraham ever compare notes in heaven on what it's like to be blessed to be a blessing?

## Think It Over

1. What might Abraham and Bonhoeffer have to say to the church in North America?

2. How has your own obedience to God blessed others? How about your church's obedience?

## In Other Words

"Only those who obey can believe, and only those who believe can obey."

—Dietrich Bonhoeffer, *The Cost of Discipleship*

## Live It Out

Watch the recent documentary *Bonhoeffer* (Martin Doblmeier, 2003), or go to the library and find one of Bonhoeffer's books to read.

# Acts of God 3

> *"Tell [your children]: 'We were slaves of*
> *Pharaoh in Egypt, but the LORD brought us*
> *out of Egypt with a mighty hand.'"*
>
> —Deuteronomy 6:21

I was rifling through my mother's silverware drawer in search of a paring knife. I settled on a likely looking candidate and began to peel the potatoes.

"Don't use that one," Mom chided. "That knife's so dull you could ride it all the way to London."

By that time I had discovered the truth for myself. But as I proceeded to peel with the sharper knife she provided, I continued to reflect on her peculiar proverb. When I asked Mom about it, she told me that it was what the women in our family always said about dull knives.

In that moment, I felt a funny sort of solidarity with that unnamed English ancestor who, in a fit of wry humor—which I like to think still runs in the family—creatively condemned her dull knife. It was a linguistic link that surprised me into a deeper sense of my connection to the past.

Perhaps something similar is going on in Deuteronomy 6:21. The previous verse anticipates that future generations may need to be reminded about the mighty act of God that forged them into a community of faith and gave them the Law as a guide to grateful obedience.

> In the future, when your children ask you, "What is the meaning of the stipulations, decrees and laws the LORD our God has commanded you?" tell them: "*We* were slaves of Pharaoh in Egypt, but the LORD brought *us* out of Egypt with a mighty hand."

I added the italics in the last quote to underscore the use of the first-person plural. Did you notice how the children's question is framed in the second person—*you*? The suggested response, however, shifts resolutely to the plural *we* and *us*. The point is unmistakable: the miraculous rescue at the Red Sea was not simply an event that happened to someone else. It happened to all of us—to every generation that belongs to the community of faith that passed through the Red Sea's birth canal that day.

The early Christians had a strong sense of that connectedness. Perhaps that had something to do with the fact that Passover celebrations always frame the story in terms of *us* (versus *them*).

When you think about being a Christian, do you ever think about the fact that you are *connected* to something much bigger and older than yourself?

North Americans in general are not very sensitive to history. Some people have even suggested we have a kind of collective amnesia! But the amnesia and individualism of our age

> ## Word Alert
> ***Passover*** commemorates the miraculous deliverance of God's people from slavery in Egypt under the leadership of Moses (Ex. 3-15). The word refers to the time when the angel of death "passed over" the houses of the Israelites but killed the firstborn son of all the Egyptian families.

can also conspire to cut Christians off from a sense of belonging to something bigger than our own beliefs. We can easily lose our sense of being connected to the larger community of faith.

So let's remember our connection to that community of faith that stretches all the way back to the banks of the Red Sea! And let's tell our children the story of God's mighty acts that delivered us from our slavery to sin.

## Think It Over

1. What helps you to feel connected to your ancestors? To your community of faith?

2. How can we help our children and new believers move from seeing the Bible as a collection of stories about other people, to a book about *us* as part of the whole family of faith?

## In Other Words

"We become a part of what once took place for our salvation. Forgetting and losing ourselves, we, too, pass through the Red Sea, through the desert, across the Jordan into the promised land. . . . We are torn out of our existence and set down in the midst of the holy history of God on earth."

—Dietrich Bonhoeffer, *Life Together*

## Live It Out

Research the date of your own baptism and celebrate it by reading Exodus 15 aloud—preferably with other members of your faith family.

# People Imperfect 4

*"In the desert the whole community grumbled against Moses and Aaron. The Israelites said to them, 'If only we had died by the Lord's hand in Egypt! There we sat around pots of meat and ate all the food we wanted, but you have brought us out into this desert to starve this entire assembly to death.'"*

—Exodus 16:2-3

Moses and Aaron must have been tempted to do a little grumbling of their own when they heard the Israelites' classic complaint. "Hold it," we can imagine them thinking. "Didn't the plagues and the deliverance at the Red Sea make any impression on you? Have you forgotten who you're dealing with here? Remember the Creator of heaven and earth, who for some reason seems to have taken a shine to you and delivered you from slavery? Who formed you into a covenant people through whom all the families of the earth will be blessed? Don't you think this God can take care of a few hunger pangs out here in the wilderness?"

Moses and Aaron may have *thought* it, but the Bible does not record them *saying* any such thing. Instead the Bible simply records God's amazingly gracious response to the people's complaint: bread and meat, manna and quail—a "table in the wilderness" (Ps. 78:19).

We should be quick to acknowledge that this is not a story about "somebody else"—to confess that we are among the "murmurers," as they're called in the King James Version of this passage. We barely make it up the bank of the Red Sea before we start complaining. To be fair, not all of those complaints are trivial. The lack of food and water is deadly serious—as are so many of the other troubles and disasters that God's people suffer in every age. But when we stand back and remember the mighty acts of God on our behalf—the suffering, death, and resurrection of Jesus Christ among them—our murmuring signifies a singular lack of gratitude and faith.

Notice that God expresses no surprise at our complaints in Exodus 16. Jesus' response to the complaining disciples in Matthew 8:23-27 is much the same. When a storm threatens to swamp their boat, the disciples wake Jesus up in a panic. (This, in spite of the fact that they've just witnessed several of Jesus' miracles.) "You of little faith, why are you so afraid?" Jesus asks matter-of-factly. Then he rebukes the winds and the waves and they sail safely on as if the whole thing were nothing but a bad dream.

If God is not surprised at our imperfections, why should we be?

So many congregations labor under an illusion of unachievable perfection. We have in our minds a fantasy—an ideal Christian community where everyone is in perfect agreement, at least most of the time. So we are surprised and disappointed when the choir gets into a tiff with the praise band, when the deacons disagree about which cause is more worthy, when certain members call into question the theological correctness of certain other members.

While I don't want to minimize the pain of such disagreements or underestimate how potentially destructive the resultant "murmurings" can be, Bonhoeffer reminds us that Christian community is not an *ideal* but a *divine* reality, and that the sooner we are disillusioned of our fantasies about a perfect and unsustainable harmony, the better off we will be. So important is this candid acknowledgment that it is God's grace that holds us together and not our own constant agreement, that Bonhoeffer identifies its lack as the "greatest danger of all." It is a danger, he says, that threatens to poison Christian community at its root by confusing it "with some wishful idea of religious fellowship" (*Life Together*).

Have you ever come home from the "mountaintop experience" of a religious retreat or service project and thought, "If only church could be like that all the time!" Understandable as it is, that sentiment stems from a dream of Christian community that sells short the "real deal." In fact, real Christian community recognizes that it's God's grace that holds a body of imperfect people together over the long haul. Our unity, our integrity, and our identity are in the cross—not in our own ability to pull off perfection.

So next time you catch yourself among the murmurers, don't be surprised. Only trust that the God who has brought us safely through the Red Sea is willing and able to prepare a table in this wilderness.

## Think It Over

1. How do Bonhoeffer's insights on the dangers of the "ideal" Christian community make you feel about your own expectations?

2. Is there ever a good reason for murmuring? For leaving a church because of a disagreement?

## In Other Words

"Disillusionment is the loss of illusion. It is not always a bad thing to lose the lies we have mistaken for the truth."

—Barbara Brown Taylor, *The Preaching Life*.

## Live It Out

Offer a compliment to someone in your congregation . . . especially if it's someone about whom you might normally "murmur."

# The Body Beautiful 5

*"[Jesus Christ] is the head of the body, the church. . . ."*
—Colossians 1:18

*"For just as each of us has one body with many members, and these members do not all have the same function, so in Christ we, though many, form one body, and each member belongs to all the others."*
—Romans 12:4-5

In her book *Traveling Mercies*, Anne Lamott describes a beautiful friend was thinking seriously about suicide—but was deterred by the fact that she really wanted to lose five pounds first.

It's hard to miss our culture's obsession with body image. We want the perfect body, and as the epidemic of eating disorders demonstrates, some of us are willing to die for it.

Maybe we can turn obsession to advantage, however, by redirecting our interest to the New Testament's "body" image for the church.

As we've already observed, the church as a body is far from perfect. Yet with all its flaws, that doesn't mean it can't be beautiful. And that doesn't mean that its head, Jesus Christ, isn't working hard to whip it into shape through the constant cajoling of the

Holy Spirit. OK, maybe the idea of the Holy Spirit as personal trainer is carrying the metaphor too far. But the point is still powerful. God is not finished with the church yet. And Jesus died to make sure that it will be perfect someday.

But there's something else that we need to learn from the New Testament's "body language." And that has to do with diversity.

In Romans 12:4-8 and again in 1 Corinthians 12:12-26, Paul reminds us that Christ's body, the church, has "many members." And just as it wouldn't do to have a body that was all arms or all feet, the church's body functions best when there is a diversity of gifts, with all the members performing the function for which they are gifted.

Sometimes we lose sight of this in our congregations. Not only do we rank gifts, giving more honor to those whose gifts are more "glamorous," but we also assume something has gone wrong when members don't act or think in similar ways. Worse yet, we find ways—consciously or unconsciously—of discouraging racial and sociological diversity in our congregations. Paul's words prod us to remember that, in the very design of Christ's beautiful body, the church, this kind of diversity is not only tolerated, but *expected*.

So what are we to conclude from all this "body language"? Simply this: *If a Christian* community *has achieved unity at the expense of diversity, then it has paid too high a price.* Even more important, it has ceased to be a truly *Christian* community.

At first glance, this kind of diversity may not be obvious in the early church. Jesus' disciples, for instance, were pretty much a group of Galilean guys. But commentator Frederick Dale Bruner suggests that there was more diversity among Jesus' disciples than meets the eye. First, consider the fact that that the list includes two sets of brothers—certainly a recipe for some tension, rivalry, and one-upmanship. Then add one Zealot (Simon) and a tax collector (Matthew). In his *Commentary* on

Matthew, Bruner observes that "a Zealot was about as far removed from a tax collector as a leftist guerilla is from a right-wing conservative." Finally, add a dash of betrayal (Judas), and you can be pretty sure that these twelve Galilean guys did not always see things the same way.

The New Testament offers further evidence that the seeds of diversity in the early church had not only been sown, but were taking root and flourishing. Roman centurions mixed it up with fishermen. Former prostitutes found their way into fellowship with doctors, lawyers, and rich businesswomen. Slaves broke bread with their former masters. Divisions of race, gender, and class began to disintegrate as those early Christians began to realize that "there is neither Jew nor Gentile, neither slave nor free, neither male nor female, for you are all one in Christ Jesus" (Gal. 3:28).

Difference is not the same as discord. In fact, difference that manifests itself as diversity is one of the things that makes Christ's body so beautiful. Let all God's people say: *Vive la différence!*

## Think It Over

1. What happens to our expectations of the church's body when we shift from perfection to beauty? To health?

2.  How healthy is your own part of Christ's body, especially in terms of diversity?

## In Other Words

"No matter how bad I am feeling, how lost or lonely or frightened, when I see the faces of the people at my church, and hear their tawny voices, I can always find my way home."

—Anne Lamott, *Traveling Mercies*

## Live It Out

Go out of your way to invite/welcome someone who would make your congregation more diverse.

# Session 1
# Foundations
## Discussion Guide

Community is central to the Christian life because it mirrors the very life of God. Believing as we do that God is triune—one God in three persons—we profess that there is community in God's own being. And since we are created in God's image, one of the characteristics of our humanity is that we are made for community. We belong together.

One of the toxic results of sin is the breakdown of community. You can see it in the first chapters of Genesis, as Adam and Eve blame each other for their sin, their roles of male and female become hardened and hurtful, and Cain kills Abel, his brother.

But God, determined to restore his broken and sinful creatures, has a plan of salvation that will once again bring people into true community with each other and with God.

Over and over again God says of the community of Israel, beginning with the patriarchs and continuing throughout the Old Testament, "I will be their God and they shall be my people." But over and over Israel fails to be God's covenant community.

In Jesus Christ, God comes to this lost world. One of his first acts is to gather around himself a community of broken and sinful people, the twelve disciples. These disciples are the new Israel who, after Christ's death and resurrection, will bring God's message of saving love to the world. They will not only *bring* it, they will *live* it as a new community of love.

Imperfect and messy as it is, the church is the community through which God continues to bring and display his love to the world. It's also the living laboratory in which we learn, with humility and care, how to love each other.

## Opening Prayer

Part of the point of meeting together is to allow the Holy Spirit to form us into a community of faith and learning. **After the group gathers, invite God's blessing** on this group of disciples by praying the following prayer in unison:

**Gracious God, thank you for leading us all here today. Come among us. Help us to love you and each other better. Teach us what it means to be your disciples. And call us ever deeper into the blessing that is Christian community. In Jesus' name we pray, Amen.**

### Option

Have a volunteer open the session with a brief prayer along the lines of the one suggested above.

## Ice Breakers

*(15 minutes—give or take)*

Since this is the first session, it's important to **take some time to get acquainted**. Distribute large, adhesive-backed nametags (or blank 3 x 5 cards) and markers. Then invite participants to write their first name *plus a symbol of a group that has been an important "community" for them*. Artistic talent is not the point, and the community may be something other than a particular congregation. It may be a group within a congregation or in the community at large. The point is to get to know something new about each other, so pick one that helps people to know something they may not already know about you.

After a few minutes for thinking and drawing, go around the group. Identify yourself, and then briefly explain your symbol and why that particular community is important for you. *Note:* **The group may want to save these nametags for use in subsequent weeks.**

If the group is already well acquainted, you may still want to go around and identify a group that has been an important "community" for you.

## For Starters
*(5 minutes)*

Invite group members to share one insight they gained from the devotional readings. It's fine if not everyone has an insight to share. Don't discuss it now, just mention it.

## Let's Focus
*(5 minutes)*

Give participants a moment to **read the following focus statement on their own.** Then, either **read it aloud together, or ask a volunteer to read it as everyone reflects.**

"The church is first and foremost a community, a collection of people who belong to one another because they belong to God, the God we know in and through Jesus. . . . It is within the church, even when the church isn't getting everything quite right, that Christian faith . . . is nourished and grows to maturity. As with any family, the members discover who they are in relationship with one another" (N. T. Wright *Simply Christian*, pp. 210-211).

## Word Search
*(20 minutes)*

Read one or more of the following Scripture passages aloud and briefly discuss the questions under each one. (You probably won't have time for all of them, so ask the group to pick the ones they especially want to cover.)

- Leviticus 26:9-13 (This passage comes near the end of a book that spells out the laws of God by which the community of Israel will be God's covenant partner.)

  What does verse 12 (a phrase that's repeated at least eighteen times in the Bible) say about God's saving intentions?

  How does it affect how we think of salvation, and how God works toward salvation?

- Mark 3:13-19
  What does Jesus' choosing the disciples say about the importance of community in God's plan?

  Why is it important that he chose twelve disciples?

- Philippians 2:1-11, 14-15
  Why do you think the author of these verses writes so passionately about "being in full accord" to the congregation at Philippi?

  When you think about these words addressed to your own Christian community, what issues come to mind?

  Does your congregation have a grumbling problem? To what extent is it healthy or unhealthy?

## Bring It Home
*(20 minutes)*

Choose *one* of these options:

### Option 1
*Note:* This option will take some preparation before the group meeting.

Have someone make a list of the twelve disciples, and then using a concordance, make a brief list of characteristics for each one. Choose some of the disciples you know most about and assign them to volunteers. Explain that their job is to simulate a discussion around the campfire between the disciples, adopting the character of their assigned disciple. Afterward, **discuss what you've learned and how it might apply to your church community.**

## Option 2
**Discuss some of these questions as time allows:**

- How would you respond to a Christian who says she prefers not to be part of a Christian community because it's so petty and hypocritical?

- Why do you think community is so important in God's plan for the world?

- Why do you think Christian community is so difficult to achieve?

- How can we grow in love and faith in such a broken and imperfect community as the average congregation?

## Option 3
No "body"'s perfect—and that's also true of Christ's body, the church. We are all sinners, saved by grace, yet we are confident that the one who "began a good work in [us] will carry it on to completion until the day of Christ Jesus" (Phil 1:6).

Pretend you are the doctor for the Christian community of which you are a part—you may think locally or globally. **Choose one of the "prescriptions" from the list below (from Phil. 2:1-11, 14-15) and describe how a dose of this "encouragement from being united with Christ" might improve the health of the body.**

- comfort from his love
- common sharing in the Spirit
- tenderness and compassion
- being like-minded
- doing nothing from selfish ambition or vain conceit
- in humility valuing others above yourselves

- looking not to your own interests, but to the interests of others
- having an attitude of self-sacrificial love (like that of Jesus)
- doing all things without grumbling and arguing
- behavior that "shines" like a star in a dark world

## Pray It Through
*(10 minutes)*

**Invite participants to raise concerns and/or thanksgivings** that they would like to include in the group's prayer. Especially remember to thank God for the Christian community of which you are a part and remember its needs. As items are raised, you may all then pray "popcorn" style. Or you may wish to write them on slips of paper and "gift" them to others in the group who are willing to voice that particular thanksgiving or request during the group's prayer. **Keep in mind that it is a powerful thing to hear others voice the prayers that are on our hearts. This is one of the most beautiful embodiments of Christian community.**

You may choose to simply **ask one person to open and close the prayer, with others using the slips of paper to prompt the prayers in between.** Remember that it is fine to simply read the request, and then leave a short period of silence for all to unite silently in prayer around each item.

**The following "template" may be used for the prayer as well:**

Heavenly Father, thank you for this time together. As you have gathered us here today, so gather now our prayers for each other, our communities, and the world.

*As each request/thanksgiving is read, leave a short period of silence for all to unite silently in prayer around that item.*

> **Word Alert**
>
> **A *template* is a pattern or a mold that helps to guide and shape something. If there are quilters in the group, they can tell you how a template works.**

*After each period of silence, a person who has been designated will punctuate the prayer with the following:*

**Leader:** Lord, in your mercy

**Group:** hear our prayer.

Eternal God, you called us to be a special people, to preach the gospel and show mercy. Keep your Spirit with us this day and in the days to come, so that in everything we may do your will and grow up in every way into him who is the head, Jesus Christ. Guide us lest we stumble or be misguided by our own desires. May all we do be for the reconciling of the world, for the building up of the Church, and for the greater glory of Jesus Christ, our Lord. Amen. (Adapted from prayer 697, *Book of Common Worship*)

# Live It Out

*(All next week)*

Pastors, elders, and other church leaders are called by God and the congregation to help build up the congregation as a community of faith and love. They provide oversight, teach, support, and, when necessary, correct behavior that hurts the community. It's a crucial, noble, and difficult task. Make a special effort to pray for your congregational leaders each day this week. Each day you might concentrate on one aspect of their task.

- Spiritual oversight
- Teaching and preaching
- Administration
- Correction and accountability
- Encouragement and spiritual counsel
- Visitation of those who are physically sick and those who are emotionally and spiritually unhealthy

Get to know Christ's body a little better and do your part to make it healthy and strong. Here are some suggestions:

- Visit your denominational website (see sidebar for tips). Read about various ministries and projects. Choose one or two each day and pray for the health of that part of Christ's body.

- Contact someone in your congregation who is active in a ministry you don't know much about. Ask him or her to tell you about their work and highlight prayer concerns. Commit to pray for those things this week, and/or volunteer to help in some other way.

---

**Web Alert**

**Most denominations have websites that are packed with information and prayer opportunities. Here are just a few:**

**www.crcna.org (Christian Reformed Church in North America)**

**www.pcusa.org (Presbyterian Church U.S.A) Note the wonderful resources under Mission Yearbook. Click on "Today in the Mission Yearbook," which includes information about a specific mission, plus a printed prayer at the end of the page.**

**www.rca.org (Reformed Church in America) Click on Mission or Reformed Church World Service for wonderful prayer possibilities.**

# Session 2
# Worship

# Word 1

*"Your word is a lamp to my feet
and a light for my path."*

—Psalm 119:105

If you've ever tried to find your way back to your campsite through the woods along a darkened path, you'll know that the psalmist is not paying God's Word an idle compliment in Psalm 119. Few of us have experienced the deep darkness that can swallow us on a dark night away from city lights. But the psalmist surely has, and just as he would cling to his lamp in the dark, so should we cling to God's Word as we make our way through life.

If the psalmist had been born a few millennia later, he might have used something else to show how crucial the Word is for Christian community. In our diet-obsessed culture, food might be an appropriate metaphor. So a twenty-first century version of Psalm 119:5 might read something like this: *Your Word is the main staple of our diet; it has the nutrients that feed our cells.*

Michael Pollan has written widely about the way North Americans eat. In *The Omnivore's Dilemma*, he points out that our diets are not nearly as diverse as we think. In fact, our entire diet has been "colonized" by one plant: corn. A careful analysis of what's on our plate reveals that almost everything we eat contains corn: corn-fed beef, corn sweeteners, corn oil, corn binders. Not surprisingly, a careful analysis of our bodies reveals something similar. Pollan writes: "Mass-spectrometer analysis on the hair and fingernails of Americans [shows] that most of the carbon [as evidenced by the signature carbon-13] can be traced back to corn. We are corn chips with legs." I've never heard a better—or scarier—illustration of the slogan "You are what you eat"!

The same is true for Christians with regard to the Word of God—in a good way! If we allow the Word to "dwell among [us] richly" (Col. 3:16), it becomes a part of who we are. It shapes us, both as individuals and as a community.

Of course, it takes more than just a twenty-minute Sunday morning sound bite for the Word of God to sink deeply into our spiritual cells. We sometimes forget that Sunday morning is not the only opportunity for worship—especially the kind of worship that arises from delving deeply into the Bible.

> ( Web Alert )
>
> **For interviews with *Michael Pollan*, go to www.npr.org. You'll find him in the archives of *Day to Day* (Nov. 27, 2003), *Fresh Air* (April 11, 2006), and *Science Friday* (Jan. 4, 2008).**

In his book *Life Together*, Dietrich Bonhoeffer points to what we might call a "threefold opportunity" for this kind of Word-based worship. The first opportunity comes to us as individuals, first thing in the morning. "At the threshold of the new day stands the Lord who made it." There is simply no substitute for this kind of "long obedience in the same direction" on an individual basis. And just as children engage in "parallel play," individual Christians who engage in this kind of disciplined encounter with Scripture *along with others in the Christian community* can gain a sense of being involved in "parallel pray."

The second setting for Word-centered worship is in small groups. Unlike a Sunday morning setting, smaller groups, including the family, give us an opportunity to discuss and ask questions. And there's less chance of getting lost in the crowd. "God has willed that we should seek and find His living Word in the witness of a brother, in the mouth of man," says Bonhoeffer.

Finally, Word-centered worship happens in the context of the congregation. The whole service is shaped around the Scripture reading for that day. Picture God's Word as the hub of a wheel with spokes reaching out into the whole service.

Many people assume that worship is a passive activity. But as we listen to God's Word and its interpretation, we are part of a Spirit-driven process that ought to engage every fiber of our being. The fact that we listen *together* reflects the fact that we are part of something much bigger than ourselves.

Here's what this process feels like from one preacher's perspective. "When I preach," says Barbara Brown Taylor in *The Preaching Life*, "sometimes I feel like Cyrano de Bergerac in the pulpit, passing messages between two would-be lovers who want to get together but don't know how." So much for passive participation!

## Think It Over

1. How do you get your diet of the Word? Did this daily reading give you any ideas?

2. Does studying Scripture feel like "worship" to you? What makes it so?

# In Other Words

"But of course, we must admit that the Scriptures are still largely unknown to us. Can . . . our ignorance of the Word of God, have any other consequence than that we should earnestly and faithfully retrieve what has been neglected?"

—Dietrich Bonhoeffer, *Life Together*

# Live It Out

One of the ways Christians experience a vibrant connection with other Christians throughout the world is through the use of *lectionaries*. (See Web Alert.) Find out whether your church uses a lectionary, and if so, which one. Ask your pastor about the pros and cons, and check out one or more of the lectionary resources listed in the sidebar.

## Web Alert

The *New Revised Common Lectionary* lists readings for Sundays and other important days of the church year. An excellent on-line site for this is http://divinity.library.vanderbilt.edu/lectionary. It includes links to two daily lectionaries as well.

*At Home With the Word is* a resource keyed to the one above that divides up the Sunday readings for study throughout the week. It is available through Faith Alive Christian Resources (1-800-333-8300; www.faithaliveresources.org) and at www.rca.org (click on Discipleship, then Daily Devotional).

# Sacraments 2

*"There is one body and one Spirit, just as you were called to one hope when you were called; one Lord, one faith, one baptism; one God and Father of all, who is over all and through all and in all."*
—Ephesians 4:4-6

*"For I received from the Lord what I also passed on to you: The Lord Jesus, on the night he was betrayed, took bread, and when he had given thanks, he broke it and said, 'This is my body, which is for you; do this in remembrance of me.' In the same way, after supper he took the cup, saying, 'This cup is the new covenant in my blood; do this, whenever you drink it, in remembrance of me.'"*
—1 Corinthians 11:23-25

Christians are never more *together* than when they are gathered around the Lord's Table or the baptismal font. That doesn't mean that we "have our act together." Far from it! The sacraments are more about what God does than what we do.

Perhaps the most powerful illustration of this in some Reformed liturgies comes just prior to the baptism of an infant. As the minister takes the child in his or her arms, he or she looks the baby in the eyes and says something like this:

> For you Jesus Christ came into the world; for you he died and for you he conquered death. All this he did for you, little one, though you know nothing of it as yet. We love because God first loved us.

As a congregation we "overhear" this good news and are reminded that our own entrance into God's family was not so much about "our deserving" as "God's love unswerving" (Johann Heermann, "Ah, Holy Jesus"). And we promise to support that person and welcome her into God's family of faith.

But the church is never more "crowded" than in the celebration of the Lord's Supper. It's not called *Communion* for nothing. There is, of course, the communion we experience as Christ feeds us with his body and blood so that we may become more and more a part of his body. But many people miss the fact that we are also simultaneously *communing* with all Christians everywhere—living and dead. See what I mean about a crowded room?

The next time your church celebrates communion, listen for the line in the communion prayer that says: "With your whole church on earth and with all the company of heaven we worship and adore your glorious name." Then, as you join your voice in the *Sanctus*, celebrate the fact that you're saying it with Mary and Martha, the disciples, the martyrs, John Calvin, and all your loved

---

**Word Alert**

The *Sanctus* is the prayer of acclamation based on the words of the angels in Isaiah 6:3, echoed in Revelation 4:8. It's followed by a blessing based on John 12:13 and Psalm 118:26. Together they read: "Holy, holy, holy Lord, God of power and might, heaven and earth are full of your glory. Hosanna in the highest! Blessed is he who comes in the name of the Lord. Hosanna in the highest!"

ones who have died and are alive in Christ. And then, in the brief silence that follows, listen as the echoes reverberate between heaven and earth.

Theologian Martha Moore-Keish helps us to shift out of our modern mindset by reminding us that the very act of "breaking bread" was a communal affair in biblical times. So to "break bread" is to share food and drink with others, not to warm up something in the microwave and eat it alone in front of *Seinfeld* reruns. And just as the communion prayer rejoices over the fact that "this grain has been gathered from many fields into one loaf, and these grapes from many hills into one cup," so Christians around the Lord's Table ache for that day when Christ's whole church "may soon be gathered from the ends of the earth into [Christ's] kingdom."

In this space we can only begin to touch on the mystery and blessing we experience in the sacraments as we focus on their *communal* dimensions. And we cannot hope to fully understand the meaning of these mysteries. That's why they are mysteries! But we can be blessed by them—and drawn closer to God and each other.

## Think It Over

1. Remember an experience of either baptism or communion that gave you a particularly powerful sense of being part of the body of Christ.

2. How does the way your congregation celebrates baptism and communion underscore the fact that it is something God does, and that it is something we celebrate together?

## In Other Words

"We may spend our whole lives learning what those sacraments mean, but the experience of them exceeds our understanding of them. Reaching out to handle God, it is we who are handled, gently but with powerful effect."

—Barbara Brown Taylor, *The Preaching Life*

## Live It Out

Find, read, and pray through your denomination's liturgies for baptism and the Lord's Supper. (See the Web Alert for help, or ask your pastor.)

### Web Alert

**Find the liturgies for the Reformed Church in America at www.rca.org under Worship. For the Christian Reformed Church, find them at www.crcna.org under Worship, and for the Presbyterian Church (USA) at www.pcusa.org under Worship.**

# Song 3

> *"Be filled with the Spirit, speaking to one another with psalms, hymns and songs from the Spirit. Sing and make music from your heart to the Lord, always giving thanks to God the Father for everything, in the name of our Lord Jesus Christ."*
>
> —Ephesians 5:18b-20

> *"Sing to the Lord a new song; sing to the Lord, all the earth."*
>
> —Psalm 96:1

Church is one of the few places people sing *together* any more. Sure, sometimes a few brave souls chime in with the National Anthem at a basketball game, but even they may lose their nerve when they get to the high part.

Solos, on the other hand, are all the rage. We tune in to *American Idol* to root (and vote) for our favorite pop singer. But woe to anyone who tries to sing along as these young hopefuls belt out their highly personalized version of familiar tunes. We can listen, but we can't do much more than appreciate those tunes from afar . . . unless we belt them out in the privacy of the shower or the car.

It's not surprising, then, that singing has become a lightning rod for controversy in so many churches. If our culture has forgotten how to sing together, why should we expect our congregations to remember?

One obvious "solution" would be to stop trying. Retire the choir. Toss out the hymnals. Let the soloists win the day. The problem is, that would be in direct violation of Scripture. "Sing!" the psalms command us in no uncertain terms. Silence is not an option, even if the best we can do is to "make a joyful noise to the LORD" (Ps. 100:1, RSV).

Why does the psalmist urge us to sing a "new" song? Is this some kind of prophetic advocacy for contemporary songs? (I like Marva Dawn's claim that a "contemporary" song is anything we happen to be singing *now!*)

A careful look at the whole psalm reveals that it does indeed celebrate something new: it anticipates the advent of God's coming to judge the world with fairness and truth. Isaac Watts set this "new song" to music in a carol based on this very psalm. "Joy to the world! The Lord is come" it announces gleefully. "Let earth receive her King!" Watts's carol leaves no doubt about the identity of that King.

Neither does Dietrich Bonhoeffer. In his book *Life Together*, Bonhoeffer describes the "new song" as "the hymn that is sung by the whole Church of God on earth and in heaven, and in which we are summoned to join. God has prepared for Himself one great song of praise throughout eternity, and those who enter the community of God join in this song."

So it is not the *style* so much as the *subject* of the song that is "new." And if Paul's words to the Ephesians are any indication, we have quite a lot of latitude in terms of style. Whether we sing "hymns, songs, or spiritual songs," the important thing is that they glorify God in Christ, and that they arise from our grateful hearts.

Of course, Bonhoeffer has something to say about this as well: "The new song is sung first in the heart, [which] sings because it is overflowing with joy. Surrender to the Word, incorporation in the community, great humility, and much discipline—these are the prerequisites of singing together."

Bonhoeffer's prerequisites could probably get us past most of our worship wars. If humility were a given in our arguments about what songs to sing in worship, most of those arguments would never get off the ground. There would still be discussions, to be sure, but they would be characterized by the same spirit of self-giving love we see in Christ Jesus. Imagine a worship committee with this motto (shamelessly adapted from Philippians 2:3-4): "Choose no music from selfish ambition or conceit, but in humility regard other people's preferences as better than your own. Let each of you look not to your own favorite style, but to the favorite styles of others."

To paraphrase another, less spiritual source: "You can't always sing what you want." But sing we must. And in view of what God has done for us through Jesus Christ, how can we help it?

## Think It Over

1. What makes for a "good" hymn, song, or spiritual song?

2. What role does a choir play in worship? How about soloists? Is there a role for both?

## In Other Words

"The Christian Church sings. It is not a choral society. Its singing is not a concert. But from inner, material necessity, it sings. . . . And where . . . it does not really sing but sighs and mumbles spasmodically, shame-facedly and with an ill grace, it can be at best only a troubled community which is not sure of its cause and of whose ministry and witness there can be no great expectation."

—Karl Barth, *Church Dogmatics*

## Live It Out

Check out the words "sing" or "song" in a Bible concordance, and reflect on what the BIble says about singing together. You can find a good online concordance at bible.crosswalk.com.

# Prayer 4

*"In the same way, the Spirit helps us in our weakness. We do not know what we ought to pray for, but the Spirit himself intercedes for us through wordless groans."*

—Romans 8:26

The little white mug that I used as a young girl has a silhouette of a boy and girl sitting at a table with heads bowed and hands folded. The words written above prompted my prayer before every meal: *I fold my hands and bow my head to thank Thee for my daily bread.*

If you were very, very blessed, you had parents who taught you to pray. Prayer doesn't come naturally. Even the disciples asked Jesus to teach them, and we're still using the prayer that he taught.

One of the most telling things about the Lord's Prayer is that it uses the first person *plural*. *Our* Father . . . Give *us* this day our daily bread . . . Forgive *us our* sins, as *we* forgive those who sin against *us* . . . Save *us* from the time of trial . . . Deliver *us* from evil. . . .

Of course we can pray the Lord's Prayer as individuals too. But even when we do so, it calls our attention to the importance of praying *together* as a Christian community.

These kinds of communal prayers show up all over the place on Sunday morning. There's a prayer of confession, a prayer for illumination, prayers of thanksgiving and intercession, and of course the Lord's Prayer. Yet we may not have given much thought to how important it is that we are praying these prayers as the collective body of Christ. When we pray together, the whole is much greater than the sum of our individual parts.

This is particularly obvious during a good prayer of confession. By "good" I mean one that brings to light *something of which we are collectively guilty*. Because it's only there that we as a body can be bathed in God's grace and receive pardon.

So, for instance, we may confess that our bargain prices for clothing are often built on the backs of poor people in Central America, Mexico, Bangladesh, and China. We may confess that our ignorance or greed has contributed to others' poverty. And if we do so, there is good news! Because the community that confesses together, gets forgiven together.

There are other moments too when we should be praying for all we're worth. One of the most overlooked is the "prayer for illumination" before the Scripture and sermon. This is the moment when the whole gathered people of God should be begging the Holy Spirit to open the community's heart to hear what God has to say that day.

And then there is the prayer that kids everywhere call the "long prayer"—the prayers of intercession and thanksgiving also known as "the prayers of the people." In the early church, the deacons often led this prayer, since they had the best sense of the needs of the community and its surroundings. I wonder if reviving that practice might help to give us a keener sense of just how powerful this community prayer effort can be.

I experienced the power of community prayer when I was staying with some Episcopal Sisters at the Community of the Holy Spirit in Manhattan. I found my way into their evening prayer service just in time to hear them praying for the people of the city, the nation, and the world with an intensity and urgency that was startling. As the service drew to a close, they continued their prayer in song. When we got to the third verse of "Now the Day Is Over," I got a vivid mental image of the city suspended over an abyss—held safe by the thread of these women's prayer: "Comfort those who suffer, watching late in pain; those who plan some evil—from their sin restrain" (Sabine Baring-Gould, 1865).

Who's to say what might have happened that night in New York if the Episcopal Sisters had not been praying for all they were worth?

## Think It Over

1. What corporate sin would you like your community of faith to confess?

2. What helps you to have a sense of urgency and intensity when your congregation is in prayer together?

## In Other Words

"The psalms teach us to pray as a fellowship. Even if a verse or a psalm is not one's own prayer, it is nevertheless the prayer of another member of the fellowship; so it is quite certainly the prayer of the true Man Jesus Christ and his Body on earth."

—Dietrich Bonhoeffer, *Life Together*

## Live It Out

Find a few friends to join you in "praying through" your local newspaper or in taking regular "prayer walks" through your neighborhood.

# Confession of Faith 5

*"Therefore God exalted him to the highest place and gave him the name that is above every name, that at the name of Jesus every knee should bow, in heaven and on earth and under the earth, and every tongue acknowledge that Jesus Christ is Lord, to the glory of God the Father."*

—Philippians 2:9-11

Whoever said, "Confession is good for the soul" was probably not thinking about standing up on a Sunday morning to say the Apostles' Creed. But that doesn't mean it doesn't apply. Confession of faith is good for the soul of the Christian community.

Let's be clear. The confession of *faith* is different from the confession of *sin*. One of the big differences is that the confession of sin is a prayer. The confession of faith, on the other hand, is a statement of belief. Both are public and, when we say them together in church, both are both communal. But their essence is quite different.

What happens during the confession of faith? Whether we use the words of one of the ancient creeds embedded in Scripture (such as Phil. 2:6-11), or a creed from the early church (such as the Apostles' or the Nicene Creed), or an

> **Word Alert**
>
> A *confession* is a formal statement of religious beliefs.

excerpt from one of the historic confessions of a particular church tradition (such as the Heidelberg Catechism), we're standing up and saying, "Hey! Count me in on something bigger than myself!"

Even as we say the words "I believe," we're really saying them with the rest of the Christian community. And that community is not just the congregation that gathers in church that particular Sunday morning. It extends across the miles and the ages and folds us into the embrace of something much bigger and older than ourselves. It is, in short, one of the most *communal* things we do as a Christian community.

Two things may trip us up: *apathy* (not thinking or caring about what we're saying) and *individualism* (thinking too much about what we're saying). The cure for the first may be as simple as another cup of coffee. The second hurdle deserves more attention, however, since it signals something that is at once more widespread and more dangerous.

Ron Byars reminds us that in North America we live in a culture where "the individual is the ultimate authority." So when North American Christians rise to repeat one of the creeds or confessions on Sunday morning, "our deep individualism makes all this *togetherness* hard for us." Some of us get tripped up by things that we don't understand, or that seem like someone else's "issue." But even as we wonder, we need to remember that the words we use to confess our common faith are not "a cacophony of simultaneous personal testimonies" or individual voices. Rather, we use words that "belong to the community of saints, including both the living and the dead."

Do you ever catch yourself wondering, "Do I really believe *that*?" while you're reciting a particular point in a creed or confession? (What does "He descended into hell" really mean, anyway?) If so, you might be surprised how many believers throughout the ages have wondered the same thing. And yet, we still call them believers. We believe—even as we occasionally have to ask God to help our unbelief (see Mark 9:24).

I'm reminded of when my dad taught me to ice skate as a little girl. After what seemed like an eternity of floundering and falling, he saw that I was within an inch of giving up. I clearly needed inspiration. So he scooped me up in front of him and we took off, winding our way through the woods along the frozen creek bed. Suddenly, with his support, I understood what it was like to ice skate! I didn't know yet how to do it on my own, but I was determined to learn.

In Africa they have a word that fits here: *ubuntu*. It means, "I am who I am because of who we all are."

## Think It Over

1. What phrases trip you up in the "confession of faith" segment of worship?

2. Has this daily reading shed some light on any doubts or questions you might have? If so, how?

## In Other Words

We believe

- that Christ's work of reconciliation is made manifest in the church as the community of believers who have been reconciled with God and with one another;

- that unity is, therefore, both a gift and an obligation for the church of Jesus Christ; that through the working of God's Spirit it is a binding force, yet simultaneously a reality which must be earnestly pursued and sought: one which the people of God must continually be built up to attain;

- that this unity must become visible so that the world may believe that separation, enmity and hatred between people and groups is sin which Christ has already conquered, and accordingly that anything which threatens this unity may have no place in the church and must be resisted . . . "

—From the Belhar Confession. This confession comes to us from the Uniting Reformed Church in Southern Africa. For more information on the context, content, and status of the Belhar, see the study guide *Unity, Reconciliation, and Justice* (www.FaithAliveResources.org).

## Live It Out

Pray through one of the creeds or confessions, pausing where necessary to pray, "Lord I believe; help my unbelief!"

Studies show that families who share at least one meal together each day tend to have significantly better relationships. Divorce rates are lower, and kids do better in school and have fewer behavioral problems. Why? It's not just that everyone eats together, chewing simultaneously. It's the interaction, the small talk, the chance to exchange those coded messages families develop. Often little rituals develop around the shared meals, from taking turns setting out the food and cleaning up to "saying grace." These things shape the family and help hold it together.

If asked to choose the most important activity of the Christian community, most of us would say worship—almost without thinking. Worship is the central activity of our life together. And like the family meal, worship shapes us and binds us together in ways that often go unnoticed. Something happens to us as a community, even as our attention is focused on the God we adore. The very activities that bind us to God in our worship—the Word and the sacraments, the singing and the praying—also bind us to each other.

## Opening Prayer

Part of the point of meeting together is to allow the Holy Spirit to form us into a community of faith and learning. **As the group gathers, invite God's blessing** on this group of disciples by praying the following prayer in unison:

**Almighty God, you built your church upon the foundation of
the apostles and prophets, with Jesus Christ himself as the**

**cornerstone. Join us together by their teaching, so that we may be a holy temple in whom your Spirit dwells; through Jesus Christ our Lord, Amen.** (Book of Common Worship, 6)

## Option
Have a volunteer open the session with a brief prayer along the lines of the one suggested above.

# For Starters
*(10 minutes)*

**Warmly welcome any who are new to your group.** Be sure to bring them "up to speed" by briefly summarizing your last session. The review won't hurt the rest of you either. Maybe someone wants to report on their experiences this past week in especially remembering church leaders in their prayers.

Also invite group members to share one insight from the daily devotions that was meaningful for them. Don't discuss it now, just mention it.

# Let's Focus
*(5 minutes)*

**Read the introduction to this session and then have someone read this focus statement aloud:**

The church is a community called to worship God. It's part of the very purpose of the church. But our worship also forms and shapes us into the kind of community God want us to be. As our worship enables us to know God through song and sacrament, preaching and prayer, God uses these very elements to sculpt us into God's own community.

# Word Search

*(20 minutes)*

Discuss the following passages from Scripture, or, if you're running short on time, choose the ones the group wants to discuss.

* Isaiah 6:1-8 (Isaiah's vision of worship around God's throne)

  How does Isaiah's experience correspond to what happens in your congregation on Sunday?

  Are there specific elements of the service that you recognize?

  This passage has an unmistakable tone of awe and reverence. Is that an important quality for Christian worship? If so, how would it shape the community?

* 1 Corinthians 14:26-33, 39-40 (Paul's teaching on worship)

  How does Paul's description of worship emphasize the communal nature of worship?

  How would the worship described in this passage shape the community that worships in this way?

* 1 Corinthians 10:16-17; 11:17-22 (Paul's teaching on the Lord's Table.)

  How did the Corinthian practice of the Lord's Supper "misshape" them? How does a proper practice of the Lord's Supper rightly shape Christian community?

# Bring It Home

*(20 minutes, or as time allows)*

**Choose one of the following options.**

## Option 1

**Sing "The Church's One Foundation" together.** (If your group is shy about singing, read the words together instead.) Pause after each stanza to ask, "What does this tell us about Christian community?"

## Option 2

**As time permits, choose from among the following questions and discuss them:**

- How does congregational singing shape the life of the Christian community? What positive effects does singing have on the community even when people disagree over the style of music in worship?

- Invite group members to share an experience in worship that helped bind them together to the church community.

- Discuss this statement: "The more worship is centered in God, the more it will create true spiritual community." Do you agree or disagree? Why or why not?

## Option 3

- Hand out copies of a typical order of worship to everyone in the group. **Go through the various parts of worship and discuss how they affect the congregation's sense of community.** How might various aspects of worship be improved to increase communal life?

# Pray It Through

*(10 minutes)*

**Invite participants to raise concerns and/or thanksgivings** that they would like to include in the group's prayer. Especially remember the worship of the community. As items are raised, you may wish to write them on slips of paper and "gift" them to someone else in the group who is willing to voice that particular request during the group's prayer.

Keep in mind that it is a powerful thing to hear others voice the prayers that are on our hearts. This is one of the most beautiful embodiments of Christian community.

You may choose to simply **ask one person to open and close the prayer, with others using the slips of paper to prompt the prayers in between.** Remember that it is fine to simply read the request and then leave a short period of silence for all to unite silently in prayer around each item.

**You may also choose to use the following "template" for the prayer:**

Heavenly Father, thank you for this time together. As you have gathered us here today, so gather now our prayers for each other, our communities, and the world.

*As each request/thanksgiving is read, leave a short period of silence for all to unite silently in prayer around that item. After each period of silence, punctuate the prayer with the following:*

**Leader:** Lord, in your mercy

**People:** hear our prayer.

Lord, we pray for the unity of your church. Help us to see ourselves as rays from the one sun, branches of a single tree, and streams flowing from one river. May we remain united to you and to each other because you are our common source of life, and may we send out your light and pour forth your flowing streams over all the earth, drawing our inspiration and joy from you. **Amen.** (From *The Worship Sourcebook,* p. 736)

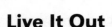

## Live It Out
*(All next week)*

During this week, take time in your daily prayers to pray for all those in your congregation who plan, lead, and support worship with their gifts and talents. Pray for people on the following list and for others:

- Worship planning team, worship committee, or individuals who plan worship
- Pastor
- Musicians
- Worship leaders other than the pastor
- Elders in their responsibility to supervise worship.

> **Web Alert**
>
> **Be sure to check out the partici-pants' section for this session on www.GrowDisciples.org for interesting links and suggestions for readings and other activities that will deepen your understand-ing of living in community.**

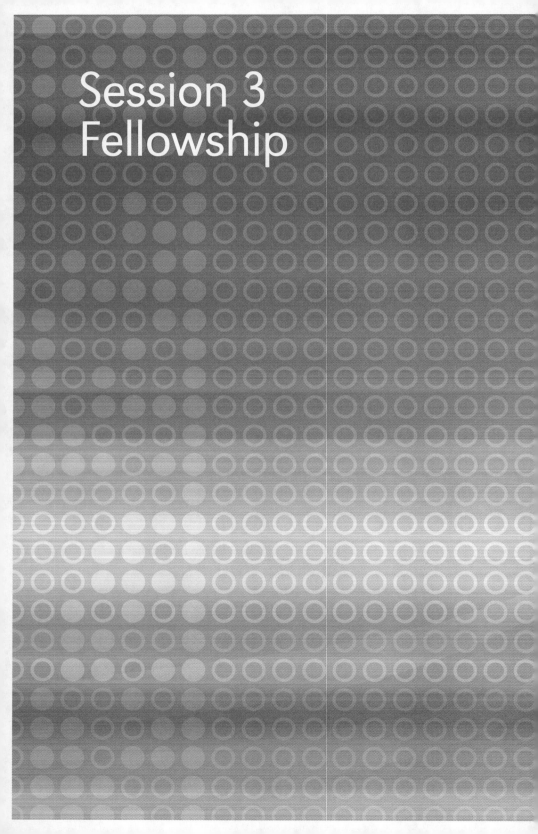

# Session 3
# Fellowship

# The Tie That Binds 1

*"My command is this:*
*Love each other as I have loved you."*
—John 15:12

Tiffany tends to gossip. In fact, she said something just the other day about Gladys, the woman sitting in the pew next to her. Gladys, for her part, can't understand why Tiffany's teenage son Jason can't wear something decent to church. Jason, a cellist in his high school orchestra, wishes the youth director wouldn't make assumptions about the kind of music young people like.

If Jesus had only told us to "love one another," it would have been hard enough. But when he added "as I have loved you," the difficulty level went through the roof. Jesus loved us all the way to the cross, after all. And in his own words, "Greater love has no one than this: to lay down one's life for one's friends" (John 15:13).

Are we willing to love that way? And at such an all-consuming cost?

These are good questions for any of us who dare to call ourselves disciples. But for the moment, let's stop worrying about how hard it is to love this way and realize instead that our love for each other is a response to the love we have already received from God. After all, *we love because [God] first loved us* (1 John 4:19).

Think of yourself as an empty glass. God's love first cleanses us, then fills us up to overflowing. The love we have for others is the direct result of what happens when "our cup overflows," to use the familiar words of Psalm 23:5.

Even though the pews of our churches are filled with imperfect people, they are also filled with forgiven people. To those who say that the church is full of hypocrites, we respond, "Of course it is—we're forgiven hypocrites who know where to go for grace!"

Have you ever traveled on an airplane that's had a really close call? Perhaps there is a prolonged period of turbulence or the pilot has to pull up suddenly and abort the landing. The moment everyone realizes the danger is past, the cabin erupts in a giddy sense of camaraderie. Perfect strangers suddenly strike up conversations. Everyone laughs at the copilot's jokes. What was once a group of individuals with nothing more in common than a destination is now a cohesive unit—bound together by a shared sense of peril and reprieve.

That's something like what binds us together as Christians. Every single one of us knows the "amazing grace" that saved a wretch like me! We've all had a very close call with sin and its consequences: death. But in Jesus Christ we've received a wonderful, unexpected reprieve from our sin, and through his resurrection, we know that our resurrection is also assured. So we get together at least once a week to celebrate. The bag lady sings songs with the bank president. We laugh at the minister's jokes—even if they're not particularly funny. We all get a little giddy on God's grace.

The Bible calls this new state of Christian reality *fellowship*. If we look closely at the Greek word behind it—*koinonia*—we realize that it is far more than just a feeling of closeness or a few minutes spent drinking coffee after church. Fellowship is what results from "having a share in" something. Christians have fellowship with Christ first (1 Cor. 1:9); as a result, we have fellowship with each other—in the overflow, one might say. We may have been individual travelers before, but now we are forged and formed into a new community of brothers and sisters in Christ.

Sometimes it's easy to lose sight of what a gift this community—this Christian fellowship—is. Maybe it's because we focus on each other's faults. Or because we sometimes forget that the church isn't a place for us to pursue our private spiritual agendas and develop our own spiritual potential. Whatever the reason, let's remember that fellowship is one of Jesus' last, best gifts to us—his disciples.

Perhaps we would appreciate our fellowship more if we were forced to live without it. Bonhoeffer reminds us of the imprisoned Paul writing with great longing for the day when he could be reunited with Christian brothers and sisters (2 Tim. 1:4; 1 Thess. 3:10)—not knowing that he himself would soon have reason to feel that same longing. Just seven years before his own imprisonment and death, Bonhoeffer wrote: "The physical presence of other Christians is a source of incomparable joy and strength to the believer" (*Life Together*).

John Fawcett had it right when he composed the hymn "Blest Be the Tie That Binds" (1782): "Blest be the tie that binds our hearts in Christian love. The fellowship of kindred minds is like to that above."

## Think It Over

1. Was there ever a time when you were prevented from enjoying Christian fellowship on a regular basis? If so, what did you miss? Was there anything you didn't miss?

2. Why is fellowship so important for Christians? Why isn't it enough to commune with God by ourselves?

## In Other Words

"When I was at the end of my rope, the people at St. Andrew tied a knot in it for me and helped me hold on. The church became my home in the old meaning of home—that it's where, when you show up, they have to let you in. They let me in. They even said, 'You come back now.'"

—Anne Lamott, *Traveling Mercies*

## Live It Out

Show your love for someone in your congregation in some tangible way—write a note, make a call, send flowers, take time to listen.

# The Flock Effect 2

*"The LORD is my shepherd, I lack nothing."*
—Psalm 23:1

Many of us have a deeply personal relationship with Psalm 23. Its words have soothed us when we're sick and consoled us at gravesides. It is, perhaps, the most intimate of all the psalms.

Maybe that's because David begins on such a personal note. "The Lord is *my* shepherd," he says. That claim is even more remarkable when we remember that it was made in a far less individualistic age.

If we knew as much about sheep as David did, however, we would also remember that sheep come in flocks. So this psalm has something to say about our life together as well. To put it another way, it's not only "*me* and the Good Shepherd" but also "*us* and the Good Shepherd."

The Bible often compares us to sheep. In my experience, this is not a compliment—though I suppose we should be thankful for small favors. My father the farmer has often remarked that the only thing dumber than a sheep is a chicken. At least the Bible pictures us in the sheepfold and not the henhouse!

Sheep may be dumb—but they're smart enough to realize that they have to stick together to survive. Oh, the panic that ensues when one of my father's small flock gets so preoccupied with the next clump of grass that she inadvertently wanders away from the flock! Her frightened "b-a-a-a!" is echoed by the answering cries of her sisters and brothers, and they run toward each other across the pasture as if they'd been separated for decades rather than minutes, and miles rather than feet.

The melodrama of their reunions always made me smile—or at least it did until my dad happened to remark that one of the lambs had been picked off by a pack of coyotes. My smile quickly faded. His observation was a stark reminder that their fears were justified. For sheep, there really is safety in numbers. So the Bible's comparison is apt. "We all, like sheep" can get into a lot of trouble when we go astray and turn each to "our own way" (Isa. 53:6).

In short, the psalm sets up a beautifully balanced picture of the life of faith. God cares for each of us as individuals (a truth that is borne out by the parable of the lost sheep in Matt. 18:12-14 and Luke 15:3-7). But God's care for us is also collective—that is, as a flock. And since whole flocks can get into trouble together (community is no insurance against collective stupidity!), the best insurance against disaster is the guidance and care of the Good Shepherd.

If you've ever watched one of those nature programs with aerial shots of herds of animals on the move, you may have noticed what, for lack of a better phrase, I'll call the "flock effect." The herd seems to move not as a collection of individuals but as one body. To paraphrase a popular proverb, "the flock is more than the sum of its sheep."

Is this true of Christian flocks as well?

In a *Holland Sentinal* article called "'Tis the Season for Creating Community," G. Corwin Stoppel describes the annual fruitcake bake at his home parish. It seems the faithful at the Episcopal

Church in Rochester, Minnesota, have been baking and selling their top-secret recipe fruitcakes for over a century. The tradition began when money was tight to help defray the expenses of the parish. But Stoppel suspects that's not the real reason they keep doing it. After all, he says, "if each of those women would put in $10 for each day they devoted to measuring, mixing, baking, and wrapping, the parish would probably be further ahead."

So why do they keep baking together? Stoppel's theory may reflect the "flock effect":

> I think they do it because they've always done it and there is great comfort in tradition. But more than that, for a week they are working together, talking, sharing secrets, telling stories about their grandchildren and great-grandchildren or feeling free enough to speak a little more openly of being lonely ever since their husband passed away and the children moved out. . . . Somehow, it's easier to open up when we're working together, wearing a little flour.

The flock effect is about more than getting a project done. And it's about more than safety and survival. Finally, it's about fellowship. It's about belonging—to Jesus Christ and to each other.

## Think It Over

1. In what way is your flock more than the sum of its sheep? (You may want to focus on a recent project or experience that drew your congregation together.)

2. How might your flock do a better job of following the Good Shepherd?

## In Other Words

"We live our Christian faith independently—not inextricably linked with other members of the Body of believers. Consequently . . . we don't experience the support that true community engenders."

—Marva Dawn, *Truly the Community*

## Live It Out

Get involved in a group effort with other Christians (a Habitat for Humanity project, a potluck, a prayer group or Bible study). If you already are involved in such a group effort, make a list of "tangible outcomes" and "intangible outcomes" that your group experienced as a result of the Holy Spirit's work among you.

# Laughing and Crying 3

*"Rejoice with those who rejoice;*
*mourn with those who mourn."*
—Romans 12:15

*"When [Job's friends] saw him from a distance, they*
*could hardly recognize him; they began to weep*
*aloud, and they tore their robes and sprinkled dust*
*on their heads. Then they sat on the ground*
*with him for seven days and seven nights.*
*No one said a word to him, because they*
*saw how great his suffering was."*
—Job 2:12-13

Have you ever noticed how hard it is to "break in" new neighbors? Sure, you can send over the Welcome Wagon, invite them for dinner, and introduce them at the block party to get things started. But there's really no substitute for going through some "stuff" together. You are neighbors in name only until you've helped each other navigate through good times and bad—weddings, funerals, babies, aging parents, promotions, pink slips, devastating diagnoses, the dreaded call in the middle of the night.

What's true of neighbors is doubly true of Christian community. There the Holy Spirit acts like superglue, making the bonds of Christian fellowship that much stronger. Again, John Fawcett gets it right in his hymn "Blest Be the Tie That Binds": "We share our mutual woes, our mutual burdens bear, and often for each other flows the sympathizing tear."

Of course, for that to happen, we have to emerge from our individual cocoons. One of the down sides of large congregations is that it's easy to remain anonymous. We can show up two minutes before the service and bolt for the car as soon as the service ends, never forming genuine bonds of Christian fellowship with others. Of course, the truly determined can spin a cocoon in any size congregation.

I remember reading about a prison in South Africa during the apartheid era. Prisoners were allowed to attend worship, but they were each herded into individual cubicles so that they could have no contact with any of the other prisoners in the "congregation." Worshipers stood in what looked for all the world like coffins set on end, seeing only the minister in a raised pulpit at the end of the room. That image has remained etched in my mind as a chilling metaphor for the way some congregations manage to be together—alone.

The book of Job tells the haunting story of a man who loses everything—wealth, children, and health—in a brutally short space of time. The quote above describes the "pastoral call" Job's three friends make when they hear the awful news. First, they cry. Then, after other traditional expressions of mourning, they sit silently beside their suffering friend—wisely not saying a word. (One might wish they'd been smart enough to *stay* silent!)

But here's something else to think about. When Job's three friends sat down with him on his ash heap, they crossed a bridge called community. In order to cross that bridge, they had to imagine what it feels like to be someone else. That kind of empathy allows us to crack open the cocoon we've been talking about. It helps us to think more about others and less about ourselves—and it is very close to the heart of true Christian fellowship.

> **Word Alert**
>
> *Empathy* is the capacity to imagine what someone else is thinking and feeling.

The gospels tell us about Jesus attending a wedding (John 2) and a funeral (John 11). It's safe to assume that he laughed with those who laughed at the former; he certainly provided practical assistance when the wine ran out! At the latter, he wept openly with the sisters of his dead friend, Lazarus. These stories show us, among other things, Jesus' own gifts of empathy. They show him entering unselfishly into their joys and their sorrows.

Of course, Jesus was not content to leave it at that. Sharing people's laughter and tears was only the first step. He called his friend Lazarus to life from the tomb. And through his own death and resurrection, he calls us from our tombs as well.

At the very heart of our faith is Jesus' act of self-sacrifice. The cross is the ultimate expression of God's love and yes—empathy—for us. It is proof positive that God not only cares about our sorrows, but is working to end them.

Think about that ultimate act of empathy the next time you are tempted to turn away from an opportunity for fellowship. Then cross the bridge of community and laugh or weep with whomever you meet on the other side.

## Think It Over

1. Think of an experience that helped you or your congregation cross the bridge of community.

2. What is there about laughing or crying with another Christian that helps forge the bond of fellowship?

## In Other Words

"Instead of explaining our suffering, God shares it."

—Nicholas Wolterstorff, *Lament for a Son*

## Live It Out

Pay a visit to someone in your congregation who might need to share a laugh or a tear. Don't worry about what to say so much as simply being there for them.

# Growing Up Together 4

*"Instead, speaking the truth in love,
we will in all things grow up into
him who is the head, that is, Christ."*
—Ephesians 4:15

The young couple had been struggling for months to adopt a child. After what seemed like an eternity of waiting, things were looking up. At last they had a name, a picture, and permission to visit the little girl they hoped would one day be their daughter.

When they arrived at the orphanage they were encouraged by the fact that the staff, though small, seemed caring and competent. The facility was warm and dry, and the babies each had their own crib.

Their first meeting with their little Hannah was full of joy and hope, tenderness and longing. But as they tried to interact with the little girl, they noticed how listless she was. On closer examination, they realized with dismay that the back of her head was flattened and bald. She could not crawl or talk. Her face had a dull, lifeless look. Hannah had apparently spent much of her first year lying on her back in her crib. As a result, she was way behind developmentally. Her new parents wondered if it was too late for her to catch up.

It was not too late, as it turned out. Hannah is now a happy, active child with an impish sense of humor and sparkling brown eyes.

Yet her parents had no guarantee of a happy ending. Hannah's father tells of the surge of hope they felt when Hannah reached eagerly for a bunch of brightly colored plastic keys that they had brought along for that first meeting. He also describes the frantic concern and growing frustration they felt in the ensuing months as they cut through the rolls of red tape that prevented them from bringing Hannah home. They knew that she was in desperate need of exercise, stimulation, and love. They also knew that every day in the orphanage was one more day that her brain, her body, and her spirit would atrophy.

We can sense the same kind of frustration in Ephesians 4. Paul pleads with the young Christians who are reading his letter to "grow up" in faith. He has just spent three chapters reminding them of the miracle of their adoption into the family of faith. The old life cannot hold a candle to the new. Yet now is not time to sit back and relax. New Christians need nourishment, exercise, stimulation, and love if they are ever going to "grow up into him who is the head, that is, Christ" (v. 15).

Though Paul is obviously concerned about these baby Christians as individuals, he also has the broader church in mind. The "body" that concerns him the most is the body of Christ, which cannot function properly if individual parts are weak and undernourished.

Like the loving father he is, Paul sets out to lavish these little ones with what they need most. For nourishment, he prescribes a steady diet of humility, gentleness, and patience (v. 2). They will need all of these if they are to "make every effort to keep the unity of the Spirit through the bond of peace" (v. 3). Unity, evidently, cannot be attained passively. Neither is it optional, given the urgency with which Paul writes about it.

Not surprisingly, exercise is Paul's next concern. Each individual Christian has been given gifts. Yet these gifts are not much good if they are left undeveloped. What Olympic figure skater ever arrived at the medal platform without thousands of hours of working out on and off the ice? Similarly, Paul urges his readers to commit themselves to a rigorous regimen of body building, remembering again that the body we are building is the body of Christ.

Without the kind of care and stimulation that Paul describes, the body cannot grow healthy and strong. Surely one of the most important gifts and responsibilities of Christian fellowship is to care for each other in this way, letting "the message of Christ dwell among [us] richly as [we] teach and admonish one another with all wisdom" (Col. 3:16).

Why do we so often act as if we can get by—either as individual Christians or as Christian communities—without sufficient attention to diet and exercise? Why don't we work harder at helping each other to grow up in faith?

Many of us are little more than toddlers in terms of our faith development. We pay little attention to prayer; we rarely read the Bible. We send our kids off to Sunday school and act as if *we* have nothing more to learn. We indulge in fits of pride, prejudice, and temper instead of disciplining ourselves to the tougher tasks of humility, gentleness, and patience.

Paul pleads with all of us—no matter what our age in the faith— to keep building up the body of Christ. His urgency is born of a parent's desperation. We have been saved "by grace . . . through faith" (Eph. 2:8). But if we don't act fast, our faith will atrophy.

We've been born again . . . and now we need to grow up! We can only do it together.

## Think It Over

1. Think of a time when someone helped you to "grow up" in faith. What effect did it have on you?

2. Think of a time when you helped someone else to do "grow up" in faith. What effect did it have on that person? On you?

## In Other Words

"Conversion cannot be thought of simply as a change of heart; it is a change of citizenship. [Christian formation] attempts to shape individuals to fit into the gospel story and to live as citizens of a new country."

—Simon Chan, *Liturgical Theology: The Church as Worshiping Community*

## Live It Out

Nurture a relationship with a young person in your congregation by paying a compliment and/or taking an interest in something he or she does.

# Holding Each Other Accountable 5

*"But the thing David had done displeased the LORD. The LORD sent Nathan to David. . . ."*

—2 Samuel 11:27b-12:1a

King David has a reputation for being "a man after God's own heart." But the reason for this is not immediately apparent in the story told in 2 Samuel 11. While Israel's army is away at war, the Commander in Chief is back at the palace playing Peeping Tom. He sees the beautiful Bathsheba—the wife of one of his most loyal soldiers, Uriah—and takes her for himself. When Bathsheba turns up pregnant, David tries to pass the baby off as her husband's by bringing Uriah home for a little unexpected R&R. When that doesn't work (because of Uriah's deep conviction that he should not enjoy the comforts of home while his fellow soldiers are still at the battle), David sends Uriah back into battle carrying his own death warrant.

It never ceases to amaze me that this story made it into the Bible— after all, David is the Old Testament's favorite king. Maybe it's God's way of getting us to understand that everyone is susceptible to sin. But if we read the rest of the story in 2 Samuel 12, we also discover that God's grace is greater than our sin.

But there is one condition. We must confess our sin—first, perhaps, to ourselves, and then to God. That's the part David needed help with. We need help too. And here's where we discover one of the most surprising and undervalued features of fellowship: accountability.

When Nathan showed up to hold David accountable for his actions, he may well have been a bit nervous. Who wants to confront a king? So Nathan decides to start with this story (2 Sam 12:1-7): A rich man stole a poor man's pet lamb and served it up to his own houseguest for supper. Enraged on the poor man's behalf, David announces: "As the Lord lives, the man who has done this deserves to die." In what is probably the best one-liner in the Bible, Nathan looks David in the eye and replies, "You are the man!"

In that instant David knew that his sins were not, in fact, secret. And he was reminded that in Israel, not even the king is above the law.

Yet the most remarkable part of this story—David's reaction to Nathan's confrontation—is still to come. After hearing Nathan out, David says simply: "I have sinned against the Lord" (v. 13).

We may appreciate David's repentant response even more if we imagine what he could have said. He could have used the old standby "Off with his head!" so popular with kings throughout the ages. Or the still more popular strategy of denial. But in fact, David chooses the more miraculous way. He simply confesses.

Could this be part of the reason David is called a man after God's own heart? Perhaps. One thing we do learn from this story is certain: *the importance of holding each other accountable in the community of faith.*

The expression "holding each other accountable" seems particularly fitting since it pictures a kind of embrace. It may feel restrictive, but ideally it grows out of a relationship of mutual care and responsibility.

Of course, there are ways to go about initiating this embrace so that it will be well received. The Bible hints at a couple of them in this story. First, the importance of prayer is implied in the phrase "the Lord sent Nathan to David." We shouldn't go running off to confront a Christian brother or sister without a lot of prayer and soul-searching first. Second, Nathan clearly gave some thought to his approach to David. The story of the poor man's lamb gave David a chance to get some perspective on his own sin by seeing it with new eyes.

Finally, Jesus tells us that if a Christian brother or sister sins against us personally, we should first "go and point out the fault when the two of you are alone" (Matt. 18:15). Only if that fails should we involve other members of the body (vv. 16-17).

If you've ever been on the receiving end of such an "embrace," you'll know how very hard it is. And it can easily be complicated by the mixed motives and/or awkwardness of the person initiating the encounter. Still, if we are truly in fellowship with one another, we voluntarily make ourselves vulnerable to this kind of mutual care and disicipline.

Holding each other accountable in Christ's body is one of the ways we express our love for one other. Who, after all, would watch a friend running toward a cliff and not try to warn him? Our embrace may not always be well received, but it's our responsibility to offer it. And when we're on the receiving end of such an embrace from our brothers and sisters, we need to consider the possibility that they are giving us one of the greatest gifts of fellowship.

## Think It Over

1. What are the risks of holding each other accountable?

2. What are the risks of *not* holding each other accountable?

## In Other Words

"The purpose of such discipline [accountability] is not to establish a community of the perfect, but a community consisting of [those] who really live under the forgiving mercy of God. Discipline in a congregation is a servant of the precious grace of God."

—Dietrich Bonhoeffer, *The Cost of Discipleship*

## Live It Out

Thank someone who has held you accountable in faith.

# Session 3
# Fellowship
## Discussion Guide

In most churches you will find a space called "the fellowship hall" or something similar. It's the place where the congregation gathers before and after the service, where coffee is served, where there's a buzz of conversation.

In the Bible, the word *fellowship* means far more than coffee time and conversation, important and enjoyable as they are. The Greek word *koinonia* that we translate as fellowship means "having a share in." As the daily readings point out, it's our sharing in Christ that makes all other sharing meaningful.

This week we will explore how we can deepen and enhance our congregational fellowship. We will share our experiences of this fellowship and the barriers that sometimes make it more difficult.

## Welcome and Prayer

Part of the point of meeting together is to allow the Holy Spirit to form us into a community of faith and learning. **Invite God's blessing** on this group of disciples with the following prayer in unison:

**Triune God, you call us into fellowship with you and with each other. In our talk and in our listening, in our earnest sharing and in our hearty laughter, in our silence and in our prayers, may we know the unity of holy love that is the source and destiny of all things—Father, Son, and Holy Spirit. Amen.**

## Option

Have a volunteer open the session with a brief prayer along the lines of the one suggested above.

# For Starters

*(10 minutes)*

**Invite group members to turn to the persons on either side and take a few minutes to share a story of a time in their life when they were especially blessed by Christian fellowship.** (You might want to ring a bell or play a chord on the piano after a few minutes to signal that it's time to switch to the person on the other side.)

## Option

Invite group members to share one insight from the daily devotions that was meaningful for them. Don't discuss it now, just mention it.

# Let's Focus

*(2 minutes)*

**Read the introduction to this session and then have someone read this focus statement aloud:**

Fellowship (*koinonia* in Greek) is the glue that binds us to one another in Christ. It can be as simple as coffee time after worship. It can be as deep as weeping with a brother or sister who is hurting, or talking about your spiritual life with another Christian. However it's experienced, Christian fellowship is not based primarily on shared interests, ethnic ties, or economic status. True fellowship binds us together because we share "one Lord, one faith, one baptism" (Eph. 4:4).

# Word Search
*(20 minutes)*

Discuss the following passages from Scripture, or, if you're running short on time, pick the ones the group wants to discuss.

- Ephesians 4:1-7, 11-16
  Reading between the lines of Paul's letter, what can we guess about the Christian community at Ephesus?

  Does your community of faith need to hear any of these encouragements? Which ones particularly impress you, and why?

- Galatians 6:1-5
  Real Christian fellowship isn't just warm feelings, it also involves a willingness to be accountable to one another. Do you think the person "caught in sin" here is guilty of some especially serious offence?

  What are the spiritual qualities of accountability here?

  Can you see this working in your church today?

- Acts 2:37-47
  What aspects of this early post-Pentecost church life especially intrigue you?

  Is this an idealized or a normative picture of the church?

# Bring It Home
*(20 minutes, or as time allows)*

**Choose one of the following options.**

## Option 1
One of the true tests of fellowship is how seriously we take the vows we make as a congregation in the sacrament of baptism. **Read the following question from a typical baptismal service:**

*The minister or elder addresses the members of the congregation and asks:*

**Do you promise to love, encourage, and support these brothers and sisters by teaching the gospel of God's love, by being an example of Christian faith and character, and by giving the strong support of God's family in fellowship, prayer, and service?**

We always respond with, "We do." But do we? How? How might we do better? How do we fulfill these promises when someone moves away?

## Option 2
**As time permits, choose from among the following questions and discuss them:**

- How deep is the congregational fellowship in your congregation?

- What can be improved, and how?

- Would you like to be accountable to your brothers and sisters in some way? Is mutual accountability, official or unofficial, actually practiced in your congregation? Why or why not? What cultural attitudes work against it? What are some practical ways it can be improved?

- In what ways is personal vulnerability a factor in genuine fellowship? Why is this hard? How can it be fostered in congregations and small groups?

## Option 3
Some in the group may be familiar with twelve-step groups like Alcoholics Anonymous and others (there may be a group that meets in your church). **Ask a volunteer to describe a typical twelve-step meeting, or invite someone who is willing to share his or her experience in such a group.** (You may want to distribute a sheet of paper to everyone listing the twelve steps.) How does the twelve-step approach foster true community? What aspects of it would be helpful in your congregation?

# Pray It Through

*(10 minutes)*

**Invite participants to raise concerns and/or thanksgivings** that they would like to include in the group's prayer. This week you might like to pray specifically for the deepening of genuine fellowship in your group and your congregation. As items are raised, you may wish to write them on slips of paper and "gift" them to someone else in the group who is willing to voice that particular request during the group's prayer. Keep in mind that it is a powerful thing to hear others voice the prayers that are on our hearts. This is one of the most beautiful embodiments of Christian community.

You may choose to simply **ask one person to open and close the prayer, with others using the slips of paper to prompt the prayers in between.** Remember that it is fine to simply read the request and then leave a short period of silence for all to unite silently in prayer around each item.

**The following "template" may also be used for the prayer.**

Heavenly Father, thank you for this time together. As you have gathered us here today, so gather now our prayers for each other, our communities, and the world.

*As each request/thanksgiving is read, leave a short period of silence for all to unite silently in prayer around that item. After each period of silence, punctuate the prayer with the following:*

**Leader:** Lord, in your mercy

**People:** hear our prayer.

You may wish to close by singing "The Servant Song" (*Sing! A New Creation,* 277) or another favorite song that talks about our life together in community.

## Live It Out

*(All next week)*

Pray each day for someone in your congregation with whom you are having a difficult time. Ask God to work in your relationship and bring you into closer fellowship with that person. Then watch for signs of God's Spirit at work answering your prayer.

If you are not already a member of some fellowship group (small group, grow group, Bible study), ask if God may be calling you into that kind of fellowship.

### Web Alert

**Be sure to check out the participants' section for this session on www.GrowDisciples.org for interesting links and suggestions for readings and other activities that will deepen your understanding of living in community.**

# Session 4
# Challenges

# Unity in the Face of Disagreement 1

"A week later his disciples were in the house again, and Thomas was with them. Though the doors were locked, Jesus came and stood among them and said, 'Peace be with you!'" —John 20:26

Jesus was not the only unexpected visitor that day. There was also an elephant in the room.

Of course, the Bible doesn't mention the elephant, but it was there just the same. It must have materialized gradually in the time between Jesus' two post-resurrection appearances recorded in John 20:19-29. There's no substitute for reading the story yourself, but here's the gist of it.

Jesus had been dead for over two days. The disciples (minus Thomas) were hiding in a house, wondering what to make of Peter's report that Jesus' tomb was empty. Mary Magdalene had come back claiming to have actually seen Jesus alive! The disciples must have wanted to believe it—but after all they'd been through, it probably hurt even to get their hopes up.

Then Jesus showed up. All of the sudden they heard his familiar, beloved voice saying, "Peace be with you." After showing them the wounds on his hands and side, he said it again: "Peace be with you."

By the time Thomas got back, Jesus was gone. (And here's where that awkward elephant starts lumbering into the room.) The rest of the disciples were ecstatic. "We have seen the Lord!" they announced. Thomas must have thought they had lost their minds, especially when they mentioned the detail about Jesus' hands and side. "Unless I see the nail marks in his hands and put my finger where the nails were, and my hand into his side," he said, "I will not believe" (v. 25).

The Bible doesn't tell us what it was like for the disciples during the week that followed. It does say that one week later, just as before, Jesus appeared again in their midst. This time, Thomas was there. And Jesus, who seemed to know that for Thomas *touching* is believing, offered the doubting disciple the evidence of his wounded hands and side.

This story has some important lessons for believers who disagree with each other—a situation you may be all too familiar with!

Can you imagine the arguments that must have taken place in the space of that week between Jesus' appearances? And these arguments weren't petty either. The very heart of the disciples' faith was at stake. On the one side were the disciples who had seen with their own eyes that Jesus was alive . . . risen from the dead! On the other side was Thomas, refusing to budge no matter how passionate or compelling their claims.

In a sermon I once heard on this passage, the preacher talked about how important it was that Thomas was still welcome among the rest of the disciples in spite of his disbelief. It tells us that the disciples who had seen and believed were

- *humble.* Though they shared their belief with Thomas, they didn't try to force it on him.

- *hospitable.* Thomas was still welcome among them in spite of their disagreements.

- *honest.* They told the truth as they understood it while patiently waiting, praying, and listening to the brother they still loved.

Christians disagree about many things. Sometimes the disagreements are petty, other times they are serious. Some even flare up into arguments that split denominations. Others simmer just beneath the surface, making everyone uncomfortable, and gradually sapping the body's vitality. Whatever the level of hostility, we can take our cue from disciples and exercise humility, hospitality, and honesty.

Three times in this story, Jesus repeats the words, "Peace be with you." The fact that he repeats them three times makes them seem less like a greeting and more like a command—a command that is even more meaningful when we remember that Jesus would have been using the Hebrew word *shalom*—indicating a state of health and wholeness. Perhaps one of the reasons for Jesus' post-resurrection appearances is so that he can say to us, his followers, in no uncertain terms: *Shalom be with you!*

> **Word Alert**
>
> **Shalom is not simply the absence of conflict, but the presence of health, wholeness, and integrity. It is still the standard greeting in the Middle East along with its Arabic equivalent, As-Salaamu alaikum.**

Does *shalom* mean there will never be disagreement in the Christian community? Not likely. But it does suggest that there can be unity, even if there are disagreements. And it calls us—no, commands us—to pray and work toward a state of health where humility, hospitality, and honesty hold sway.

## Think It Over

What would happen if people in your congregation applied humility, hospitality, and honesty to those areas where there is disagreement?

## In Other Words

A classic "Peanuts" cartoon by Charles M. Schultz shows Snoopy sitting on his doghouse, tapping away at his typewriter. He's writing a book on theology. Its title? "Have You Ever Considered You Might Be Wrong?"

## Live It Out

Pray about a disagreement that is disturbing the peace of your Christian community. Look for ways you can be humble, hospitable, and honest in the situation.

# Faithfulness in the Face of Idolatry 2

*"[Aaron] took what they handed him and made it into an idol cast in the shape of a calf, fashioning it with a tool. Then they said, 'These are your gods, Israel, who brought you up out of Egypt.'"*

—Exodus 32:4

Few of us feel the urge to worship golden calves these days—unless, of course, they are the kind we can acquire with the aid of a running track and a tanning booth!

Yet the urge to "put [our] trust in an idol or swear by a false god" (Ps. 24:4) is a fairly timeless tendency, especially in the church. We forget that our worshiping community is about God and begin to assume it's about us. We substitute patriotism or the budget or the beautiful new building for God. Sometimes we even start worshiping the pastor, turning our church into a personality cult.

Denominations can be guilty of this kind of thing too. We start out with the best of intentions, setting goals for growth and throwing all of our energy into new church starts. Yet at some point we may begin to notice that our efforts are motivated at least in part by the fear of shrinking into insignificance. Or we begin to neglect the care and feeding of the sheep we already have, in our obsession with bringing more sheep into the fold. Perhaps achieving our growth goals becomes an excuse for cutting corners and compromising who we are.

Notice that in many cases, the things that seduce us are not evil in and of themselves. (After all, who doesn't want a good pastor? Who can argue with church growth?) So we need to remind ourselves that making anyone or anything other than God the object of our devotion is idolatry.

> **Word Alert**
>
> *Idolatry* is worshiping something that isn't God as if it were God.

It's a violation of God's command "You shall have no other gods before me" (Ex. 20:3).

In addition to begin wrong in itself, idolatry spells death for Christian community. It works like a slow-acting poison. Sometimes we don't even feel it coming on, but in the end, idolatry kills community.

The story of the golden calf in Exodus 32 makes that pretty obvious.

Moses has been up on the mountain a little too long, visiting with a God who is clouded in mystery. So the impatient Israelites lobby Moses' brother, Aaron, to make them a god that will be much easier to keep an eye on. Aaron passes the plate, melts down their gold jewelry, pours it into a mold, and presto—"out came this calf!" (Ex. 32:24).

The people's reaction to their newly minted god shows how quickly our allegiances can shift from the real to the fake. Their outburst includes some astonishing revisionist history: "These are your gods, O Israel, who brought you up out of the land of Egypt!" (v. 4). Though they can still taste the salt of the Red Sea on their lips, they quickly forget the One who really rescued them from their Egyptian masters.

"What were they thinking?" we ask, shaking our heads. And yet, don't we sometimes yield to temptation with the taste of the communion elements still on our tongue?

Notice how quickly the people's unfaithfulness drives wedges between segments of the community. The people and Aaron are now *over against* Moses and God. Meanwhile, up on the mountain, God and Moses are not getting along very well either. God knows what the people are up to, and seems anxious to disown them. "*Your* people," God announces to Moses, "whom *you* brought up out of Egypt, have become corrupt" (v. 7). Finally, in a fury, God threatens to destroy the people and start over again with Moses (v. 10).

By means of three persuasive arguments (which boil down to "All that work for nothing?" "What would the neighbors say?" and "You promised . . ."), Moses actually persuades God to change course, avoiding this worst-case scenario. But the people must pay a price for their idolatry. And it isn't pretty. Seventeenth-century preacher Joseph Hall, describes how Moses "burns and stamps the calf to powder and gives it [to] Israel to drink, that they might have it in their belly, instead of their eyes . . . that, instead of going before Israel it might pass through them, so the next day they might find their god in their excrements" (*Contemplations of the Historical Passages*, Book V).

A grim end to a golden beginning.

All of our attempts to push God aside are doomed to the same humiliating failure. Eventually, our "false idols" prove to be just that—false. And we find ourselves estranged from each other, from God, and from our best selves.

How quickly we forget the One who brought us through the Red Sea—through the waters of baptism. How quickly we forget the One who "so loved the world that he gave his one and only Son, that whoever believes in him shall not perish but have eternal life" (John 3:16).

There's really no substitute for a God like that!

## Think It Over

1.  What or who are the "golden calves" in your life? In the life of your community?

2.  Why is it so easy to idolize good things?

## In Other Words

"If our Lord is Jesus, then our service of others will be empowered and inspired and directed by him. If we make ourselves our own lords, then we will try to serve ourselves out of our own abilities and for our own ends."

—Marva Dawn, *Truly the Community*

## Live It Out

Make a "top ten" list of things you are most proud of in your church (either at the level of the congregation or denomination). Then ask, "Are any of these in danger of becoming idols?

# Forgiveness in the Face of Hurt 3

*"So [the younger son] got up and went to his father. But while he was still a long way off, his father saw him and was filled with compassion for him; he ran to his son, threw his arms around him and kissed him. The son said to him, 'Father, I have sinned against heaven and against you. I am no longer worthy to be called your son.'"*

—Luke 15:20-21

"Mom, Melissa hit me!" wailed the aggrieved voice from the family room.

The newspaper stirred slightly and the weary mother behind it sighed. Was it worth walking to the other room to referee? Why couldn't they work these things out for themselves? Or better yet, not get into them in the first place? She opted to stay where she was.

"Melissa, did you hit your brother?" she called.

"Yes, but he . . ."

"Did you hit your brother?"

"Yes."

"Then tell him you're sorry."

Silence. The mother lowered the paper and listened until at last she heard the mumbled apology. Good, she thought, going back to her reading.

But before long, the aggrieved voice piped up once more: "Mom, I don't think she meant it!"

Forgiving someone is much easier if we're *sure* the person is sorry. But more often than not, it's hard to tell. Even if she's said the words, we can never be sure it's more than lip service.

The older brother in the story of the prodigal son is in a similar bind. He may have it even worse, since if we read the story carefully, he never actually hears his brother's eloquent confession: "Father, I have sinned against heaven and against you. I am no longer worthy to be called your son" (Luke 15:21).

Put yourself in the elder brother's shoes. "Junior" had insulted their father and convinced him to cough up his half of the inheritance. Then he disappeared to do goodness-knows-what. Meanwhile he, the obedient older brother, had been working "like a slave" on his father's farm. In fact, he'd been coming in from the field when he heard the sounds of a serious party coming from the house. Who was it for? Why hadn't he been invited?

He'd asked one of the servants what was happening. And as if that weren't humiliating enough, the servant had announced the "good news": Junior was back, and Dad had fired up the barbecue pit and hired a band.

We're quick to criticize the older brother for his arrogant and unforgiving attitude—overlooking the detail that he has no certain knowledge of his brother's repentance. From his perspective, the prodigal brother seems to have just shown up, acting as if nothing is wrong. How would you feel?

Angry, for a start. Maybe even hateful. What's more, since those feelings had probably been simmering for some time, the welcome-home party might just bring them to a rolling boil.

In a perfect world, every act of forgiveness would be preceded by a sincere apology. But the world does not always work that way. Not even the Christian community works that way. Victims of abuse have to go on living with or without the repentance of their abusers. Sometimes death steps in and precludes the possibility of repentance, and the living victims are left with nowhere to carry their rage. What's the alternative to rage and resentment?

Jesus showed us a more excellent—though by no means easier—way. As he was dying on the cross, he prayed on our behalf, "Father, forgive them, for they do not know what they are doing" (Luke 23:34). Notice that his forgiveness is not contingent upon our realizing the scope of our crime or on our asking for forgiveness. He simply forgives.

Of course, forgiveness isn't easy, and sometimes it takes a long time to get there. What's important is not that we've arrived at fully forgiving someone who hurt us, but that we're on the way with God's help.

But just as forgiveness is a requirement in Christian community, so is a candid acknowledgement of our sin—whether as individuals or as a body. While we cannot force others to confess their fault, we must take responsibility for ourselves.

And just as the prodigal son confesses his sin to his father and is thus restored to the whole family, so we as individuals should to confess our sins to a trusted Christian brother or sister.

## Think It Over

1. Have you ever been held hostage by hate over a situation in your congregation? What did it feel like? How did it affect the larger community of faith?

2. How do you handle it when someone apologized but you are unsure if he or she really means it? If someone does not apologize at all?

## In Other Words

[When mutual confession happens] the last stronghold of self-justification is abandoned. The sinner surrenders . . . and is no longer alone with [his or her] evil. Now [he or she] stands in the fellowship of sinners who live by the grace of God in the Cross of Jesus Christ.

—Dietrich Bonhoeffer, *Life Together*

## Live It Out

Seek out someone you have wronged and tell him or her that you are sorry.

# Faithfulness in the Face of Tragedy 4

*"Though the fig tree does not bud and there are no grapes on the vines, though the olive crop fails and the fields produce no food, though there are no sheep in the pen and no cattle in the stalls, yet I will rejoice in the LORD, I will be joyful in God my Savior."*
—Habakkuk 3:17-18

Sometimes it's personal. Two teenagers have their date—and their lives—permanently interrupted by a drunk driver. . . . A sunny afternoon on a snowmobile turns suddenly tragic. . . . A young mother struggles to help her six-year-old face the fact that he will probably not live to be seven. . . . Tragedy strikes with ruthless finality, and a Christian community reels from the blow.

Sometimes tragedy's sucker punch strikes from a distance, but we must still try to come to terms with its consequences. A desperate young man mows down random classmates at a college campus. . . . A hurricane brings the most powerful nation on earth to its knees in a matter of hours. . . . A tsunami swallows up 283,000 lives half a world away. . . .

After the Indonesian tsunami of 2004 the American airwaves were clogged with talk-show hosts, preachers, and commentators all struggling to answer one question: *Why?* Their explanations—

ranging from the arrogant to the absurd—illustrated the age-old tendency to try to make sense of senseless tragedies.

The Bible actually gives us permission to ask why. We don't have to read very far in the book of Job or the psalms to discover that we may have a lot more latitude in railing against the Almighty than we realize. Job's demands for a divine explanation for his suffering culminate in his serving God with a virtual subpoena: "I sign now my defense—let the Almighty answer me!" (Job 31:35). And Jesus himself used the words of the psalmist when his own questions reached their final crescendo on the cross: "My God, my God, why have you forsaken me?" (Ps. 22:1).

It is one thing to ask why; it is another to expect that we will understand the explanation. This seems to be the point the prophet Habakkuk has reached in the passage quoted above. But it's important to recognize that he has not come to this point quickly or easily. The Babylonians are poised to devour the covenant community, and the prophet plies God with a series of painful questions:

How long, LORD, must I call for help, but you do not listen? Or cry out to you, "Violence!" but you do not save? Why do you make me look at injustice? Why do you tolerate wrongdoing? Destruction and violence are before me; there is strife, and conflict abounds (Hab. 1:2-3).

If there had been talk shows in Habakkuk's day, someone would surely have broadcast an overconfident explanation for Israel's suffering. But the prophet, mercifully spared from the temptation to tune in, retires to a nearby watchtower to think and to discern what God has to say. "I will stand at my watch," he says, "to see what [God] will say to me, and what answer I am to give to this complaint" (Hab. 2:1).

God does not immediately answer Habakkuk's questions. But God does give him a promise. Picking up on Habakkuk's "watchtower" metaphor, God tells him to keep straining his eyes toward the explanation he seeks—to keep his pencil poised so that when the vision comes, he can write it down in letters so large that even someone running by will be able to read them. (And you thought billboards were a modern invention!) But while Habakkuk waits for the answers he so longs for, he—and all the righteous—must "live by their faithfulness" (vv. 1-4).

Maybe that sounds like a cop-out. But there is real reassurance here for Christian communities paralyzed by tragedy. When innocent lives are cut short and when doubt and frustration threaten to fray our faith threadbare, God's words to Habakkuk may be just what we need to hear. We are to live by our faithfulness, putting one foot in front of the other on the path of righteousness, even though it may seem like there's nothing in it for us.

Christians sometimes assume that their faith entitles them to a free pass from suffering and tragedy. But the Christian life is more than "let's make a deal." If Job and the psalms and Habakkuk don't make that clear, then surely Jesus' words, "take up your cross and follow me" do.

In times of tragedy, one of the most important ways the Christian community can minister to each other and witness to the world is to faithfully *wait*—knowing that "there is no place where earth's sorrows are more felt than in heaven." So we wait, knowing that the vision, when it comes, will be big as a billboard.

## Think It Over

1. Why do we feel the need to offer "answers" in tragic situations?

2. Would you rather have a promise or an explanation? Why?

## In Other Words

"View the present through the promise, Christ will come again.
Trust despite the deepening darkness, Christ will come again.
Lift the world above its grieving through your watching and believing
in the hope past hope's conceiving: Christ will come again."

—Thomas H. Troeger From *Borrowed Light* © 1994, Oxford University Press, Inc. Used by permission. All rights reserved.

## Live It Out

Make a list of things people say to each other at funeral homes. Do any of them try to explain too much?

# Honesty in the Face of Apathy 5

*"'You say, "What a burden!" and you sniff at it contemptuously,' says the Lord Almighty."*

—Malachi 1:13

Have you ever felt like you were just "going through the motions" at church? Many church leaders feel that way.

> Janet found herself dreading the Christmas season. It was bad enough that she had so many responsibilities at work and at home. And how many years had she been in charge of the Christmas program? It was just getting to be too much. . . .

> Gary groaned as he sat in the back pew at the congregational meeting. He'd been elected to yet another term as elder. His wife was going to explode. . . .

> Pastor Joan was conducting her fifth funeral in three weeks. She was exhausted. And it's not as if the sermon for Sunday were going to write itself. But she couldn't worry about that now. She had to concentrate to make sure she didn't say the wrong name during the service. . . .

All three leaders in the examples above are suffering from what we call "burnout" these days. But leaders are not the only ones who are susceptible. This kind of apathy can creep up on all of us—even entire congregations. Whether we are, as the King James translation puts it, "weary in well doing" (Gal. 6:9; 2 Thes. 3:13), or simply numb to a story we have heard too many times, all of us have seasons when it feels like we are simply going through the motions of our faith rather than celebrating a vibrant reality.

> **Word Alert**
>
> *Apathy* is a lack of feeling, interest, or concern.

The priests in Malachi's day knew the feeling. But for them, apathy had deteriorated into downright hypocrisy. Instead of offering the very best animals as sacrifices, they routinely substituted animals that were blind, lame, or sick. They may have succeeded in fooling themselves, but they weren't fooling the prophet Malachi—and they certainly weren't fooling God.

Picture Malachi as a stern but loving grandmother who sometimes has to sit us down and give us a good talking-to. She may sound angry—indeed, she *is* angry! But she knows we can do better. She knows we need to be reminded of who we are and *whose* we are. We are part of a family, after all, and she is not about to let us forget it.

In this "grandmotherly" guise, the prophet first gets the priests' attention by letting them know that he sees—and hears!—exactly what they are up to. Then he throws in a few threats, the most colorful of which is that if they don't shape up, God is going to cover their faces with the dung of their impure offerings! (Mal. 2:3). But then Malachi's tone turns almost tender as he reminds them of their calling (vv. 4-9). True priests, Malachi tells them, are characterized by reverence, integrity, and trustworthy teaching. Instead of the stick, Malachi now offers the carrot, hoping that they will reach for it with all the love and energy and integrity they had felt in the beginning.

Malachi's plea to the fallen priests may remind us of all of the priests, ministers, and other trusted church leaders who have betrayed the most vulnerable members of their congregations. But it would be a mistake for us to think Malachi's words are only meant for others. They are an important reality check for all of us who find ourselves sighing, "What a burden!" as we look toward Sunday morning.

One of the most serious threats to Christian community is the tendency to start "going through the motions." At the same time, Christian community is, in a way, the best medicine for fighting such apathy. Here's why.

As hard as they are to hear, Malachi's words are spoken in love. Even more important, they are spoken from within the community of faith. There is a sense in which we must all be Malachi for each other. That is, we need to be alert for "the word that sustains the weary" (Isa. 50:4). We need to share leadership responsibilities so that people get a chance to rest and be refreshed in their faith. We need to listen for the voices from the margins of our faith community because they may have a way of telling the "old, old story" that makes it new again.

And if, as individuals or as a body, we slip into apathy—or worse, from apathy to outright hypocrisy—then we may need to give each other a loving reminder of who and *whose* we are.

## Think It Over

1. What about church makes you weary?

2. What are the risks of trying to be a Malachi by yourself?

## In Other Words

"Now, when I know the Sabbath is near, I can feel the anticipation bubbling up inside of me. Sabbath is no longer a good idea or even a spiritual discipline for me. It is my regular date with the Divine Presence that enlivens both body and soul."

—Barbara Brown Taylor, *Leaving Church*

## Live It Out

Find a way to offer "the word that sustains the weary" by helping and supporting someone in your congregation who needs to be refreshed.

# Challenges
## Discussion Guide

It may seem that living together in Christian community ought to be simple. After all, we are bound together by God's love in Christ, united by the Holy Spirit in one baptism, and joined in one faith. But of course it's not that easy. A quick reading of the New Testament will convince us of that.

Living in community is always messy because we are messy people. Although we are united in Christ, pride, vanity, envy, and innumerable other sinful habits tend to get in the way.

But that very messiness points us to God's purpose in Christian community. It's one of the most important means by which our lives are transformed by the Holy Spirit.

I remember someone likening Christian community to the process of polishing stones. You take a bunch of ordinary stones and put them in a barrel with a special medium. The barrel turns and turns for days or weeks, rubbing the stones against each other until they become smooth and shiny.

That's a lot like what happens in Christian community. We rub against each other with our dull surfaces and sharp edges as the solution of Word and Spirit cleanses and burnishes us. God uses the very challenges of Christian community to teach us what it means to love one another.

## Welcome and Prayer

*(10 minutes—give or take)*

Part of the point of meeting together is to allow the Holy Spirit to form us into a community of faith and learning. **Invite God's blessing** on this group of disciples with the following prayer:

**Gracious God, who knows our needs even before we ask, come among us during this time of study and fellowship. As we think about the things that challenge us as a community of faith, help us to feel your Spirit teaching us and your hand guiding us so that we may be your faithful disciples. Through Jesus Christ, our Lord, Amen.**

### Option

Have a volunteer open the session with a brief prayer along the lines of the one suggested above.

## For Starters

*(5 minutes)*

Invite group members to share one insight from the daily devotions that was meaningful for them. Don't discuss it now, just mention it.

## Let's Focus

*(2 minutes)*

**Read the introduction to this session and then have someone read this focus statement aloud:**

In *Life Together*, Dietrich Bonhoeffer tackles the disappointment we often feel when Christian community does not live up to our dream of perfection:

> Even when sin and misunderstanding burden the communal life, is not the sinning brother still a brother, with whom I, too, stand under the Word of Christ? Thus the very hour of disillusionment

with my brother becomes [a blessing], because it so thoroughly teaches me that neither of us can ever live by our own words and deeds, but only by that one Word and Deed which really binds us together—the forgiveness of sins in Jesus Christ. When the morning mists of dreams vanish, then dawns the bright day of Christian fellowship (pp. 28-29).

# Word Search

*(20 minutes)*

**Read one or more of the following Scripture passages aloud and discuss the questions that follow (or your own questions).**

- Acts 15:36-41
  Paul and Barnabas have a serious disagreement over Mark. What is the issue?

  How would you explain the different approaches of Barnabas and Paul?

  Were they right to separate?

  Have you had a similar experience in Christian community? (Make sure to read the rest of the story in Colossians 4:10.)

- Ephesians 4:14-16
  What is the infantile activity Paul describes here?

  What do you imagine it actually looked like?

  Can you relate it to your own experience in community?

  How does "speaking the truth in love" help us to "grow up?"

- 1 Corinthians 1:3-13
  This passage is the beginning of a letter the apostle Paul wrote to the troubled church in Corinth. What are some of the challenges this community of faith is dealing with?

What do you think Paul means by telling them to "agree with one another?"

How would they go about doing that?

If Paul were writing a letter to your community of faith, what challenges might he address?

# Bring It Home
*(20 minutes, or as time allows)*

**Choose one of the following options.**

## Option 1
In a reflection called "We All Need Mending," Susan Cooke Kittredge writes about how mending is different from fixing. **Read the following quote, then discuss what needs to be mended in our community of faith.**

Mending doesn't say, "This never happened." It says instead, as I believe the Christian cross does, "Someone or something was surely broken here, but with God's grace it will rise to new life." (From NPR's *This I Believe* series produced by Jay Allison; aired February 3, 2008)

> **Web Alert**
>
> **You can listen to Susan Cooke Kittredge's entire essay at www.npr.org; enter the author's name in the search box.**

## Option 2
**As time permits, choose from among the following questions and discuss them:**

• Describe a challenging or difficult experience of Christian community through which you experienced spiritual growth. How did it help you grow?

- Take another look at the Bonhoeffer quote under "Let's Focus." Why does he say that disillusionment can be good? Describe a time when you felt disillusioned with the Christian community. How did you deal with it?

- Some kind of conflict is inevitable in any Christian community. What are some healthy and unhealthy ways of handling it?

## Option 3
**Invite the group to come up with a top ten list of challenges to Christian community as follows:**

- Distribute 3 x 5 cards and ask everyone to write down one or two challenges. (They may use those covered in the devotions for the week or add their own.)

- Collect the cards and write the suggestions on newsprint or a board.

- As the leader reads from the list, invite everyone to vote for three.

- The top ten will emerge according to the number of votes each challenge receives. Write these on a separate sheet.

**Then discuss a few of the top challenges.** What makes them so difficult? What's the best way of responding to them as individuals and as a community?

# Pray It Through
*(10 minutes)*

**Invite participants to raise concerns and/or thanksgivings** that they would like to include in the group's prayer. As items are raised, you may wish to write them on slips of paper and "gift" them to someone else in the group who is willing to voice that particular request during the group's prayer. Keep in mind that it is a powerful thing to hear others voice the prayers that are on our hearts. This is one of the most beautiful embodiments of Christian community.

You may choose to simply **ask one person to open and close the prayer, with others using the slips of paper to prompt the prayers in between.** Remember that it is fine to simply read the request and then leave a short period of silence for all to unite silently in prayer around each item.

**You may also use the following "template" for the prayer:**

Heavenly Father, thank you for this time together. As you have gathered us here today, so gather now our prayers for each other, our communities, and the world.

*As each request/thanksgiving is read, leave a short period of silence for all to unite silently in prayer around that item. After each period of silence, punctuate the prayer with the following:*

**Leader:** Lord, in your mercy

**People:** hear our prayer.

If your group likes to sing and is familiar with the song "Healer of Our Every Ill" by Marty Haugen (*Sing! A New Creation,* 205), you may want to end your time of prayer by singing it together.

## Live It Out
*(All next week)*

Choose one of the "challenges" discussed this week that seems particularly relevant to your life or your community and make it the focus of your prayers, asking God to give you fresh ways to make this challenge into a point of spiritual growth.

> **Web Alert**
>
> **Be sure to check out the participants' section for this session on www.GrowDisciples.org for interesting links and suggestions for readings and other activities that will deepen your understanding of living in community.**

# Session 5
# Witness

# This Little Light of Ours 1

*"You are the light of the world. A city on a hill cannot be hidden. Neither do people light a lamp and put it under a bowl. Instead they put it on its stand, and it gives light to everyone in the house. In the same way, let your light shine before others, that they may see your good deeds and glorify your Father in heaven."*

—Matthew 5:14-16

The news was chillingly familiar: a lone gunman had opened fire in a schoolroom and snuffed out the lives of five children before taking his own life. This kind of news shocks but does not necessarily surprise us.

Yet the story of Charles Carl Robert IV's act of aggression against his Amish neighbors on October 2, 2006, still has the power to surprise in one respect: the Amish community responded with *forgiveness*. One Amish man held Robert's sobbing father in his arms, reportedly for as long as an hour, to comfort him. Soon after, the Amish Christians set up a charitable fund for the killer's family. In response to this outpouring of forgiveness, Robert's widow, Marie, wrote:

> Your love for our family has helped to provide the healing we so desperately need. Gifts you have given have touched our hearts in a way no words can describe. Your compas-

sion has reached beyond our family, beyond our community, and is changing our world. . . .

The widow's words echo something Jesus said about the powerful witness of the Christian community. "You are the light of the
world," he told the disciples and the gathered people (Matt. 5:14).

In October 2006, the world could hardly believe how bright that
light was. Some responded with disbelief, others with anger. How
could anyone forgive so quickly and so completely? asked the commentators. Doesn't such a reaction make light of the problem of
evil? No, the Amish insisted. It is simply what Christians are called
to do by the man who used his dying breath to say, "Father, forgive them; for they do not know what they are doing" (Luke 23:34).

The idea of witnessing often brings to mind the work of individual
missionaries or evangelists. Yet the Amish example and Jesus'
words about letting our light shine remind us that the whole Christian community is called to be a witness to God's grace as well.

The communal nature of this call is even more obvious when
we notice that Jesus is speaking in the plural in the Sermon on
the Mount: "You [all of you!] are the light of the world. . . ." The
disciples represent the whole of the Christian community. So, as
Frederick Dale Brunner says in his Commentary on Matthew, when
Jesus tells them they are the light of the world, he means that

> there is something about the way Christians "are," about
> the way they live together and talk about each other, and
> about the way they relate to the not always friendly sur-
> rounding world that is meant to catch the world's atten-
> tion, that is, to cause people to ask, "What kind of people
> are these?" "Who *are* these people?"

"Who *are* these people?" is precisely the question everyone was asking after the Amish community forgave the man who killed their children. In that one stunning act of collective compassion, they helped the world to see what it means to be a Christian. They taught the world how to stop revenge in its tracks. They showed the world "the most excellent way" (1 Cor. 12:31).

But forgiveness is not the only way the Christian community is called to bear witness. In the next few daily readings, we will look at several other areas that offer powerful opportunities for us to let our light shine. All of them involve a *substitution* of sorts. In order to make room for the good thing, we must get rid of the bad thing. So just as forgiveness replaced revenge in the Amish community's witness, we'll explore what it looks like when

- generosity replaces greed.
- justice replaces injustice.
- reconciliation replaces divisions of race, gender, and class.
- care for creation replaces reckless disregard for the world's resources.

This view of Christian community is as countercultural as it gets. And it is a call to a way of being that demands a great deal of us. But when the church remembers this part of its witness, this little light of ours will become the beacon that shows the world the way.

## Think It Over

1. How would you describe your Christian community's *collective* witness? Where are you doing well? Not so well?

2. What did the Amish Christians give up when they forgave? What did they gain?

## In Other Words

"Violence stands condemned by its failure to evoke counter-violence."

—Dietrich Bonhoeffer, *The Cost of Discipleship*

## Live It Out

Sit down with a couple of others from your congregation and brainstorm together about ways your church could let its light shine in your community.

# Giving Ourselves Away 2

*"But to you who are listening I say: Love your enemies, do good to those who hate you, bless those who curse you, pray for those who mistreat you. If someone slaps you on one cheek, turn the other also. If someone takes your coat, do not withhold your shirt. . . . Do to others as you would have them do to you."*

—Luke 6:27-29, 31

The story never said whether Julio Diaz is a Christian. But if he isn't, he was sure doing a fine imitation of one the day he took his would-be mugger out to dinner.

**Web Alert**

You can listen to a recording of Julio Diaz telling his story at www.npr.org. Go to Morning Edition's Archives for March 28, 2008, and click on "A Victim Treats His Mugger Right."

Diaz was on his way to his favorite diner one night in the Bronx when he was held up at knifepoint by a teenage boy. Diaz gave the kid his wallet, but then offered him his coat as well. "If you're going to be robbing people for the rest of the night," Diaz told the boy, "you might as well take my coat to keep warm."

It was the beginning of a beautiful—if unusual—encounter. The two ended up at the diner for a bite to eat. As they ate, a parade of people came by to greet Diaz. The boy was puzzled and asked him if he owned the place. "No," Diaz told the teen. "I just eat here a lot."

> He says, "But you're even nice to the dishwasher." Diaz replied, "Well, haven't you been taught you should be nice to everybody?" "Yeah, but I didn't think people actually behaved that way," the teen said (from a *StoryCorps* transcript produced for *Morning Edition* by Michael Garofalo).

When the bill came, Diaz had to ask for his wallet back to pay the bill. The boy handed it over. As Diaz took care of their tab, he pulled out a $20 bill and gave it to his new friend. But then he asked for something in return: the boy's knife. He gave it to him, and the two went their separate ways . . . both richer for the experience.

If we step back from this amazing story for a moment, one of the things we notice is that Julio Diaz "disarmed" his would-be mugger in more than one way. Long before Diaz talked the boy into giving up his knife, he disarmed him with kindness. It's likely that the second "disarmament" would never have happened without the first.

As powerful as this story is on an individual level, imagine what might happen if whole churches—or even the whole church—took Jesus' commands in Luke 6 (and Matt. 5) more seriously? (Again, his words are directed to the Christian community as a whole, and not just to individuals within it.)

Maybe it would look something like the small, urban congregation in New Jersey that was down to 63 members, wondering whether to close its doors. At a congregational meeting, the members made a list of what they had to offer. First on the list, of course, was the gospel. Second was meeting space. Neighborhood groups were finding it increasingly difficult to find a place to meet that didn't require a big fee and a bigger commute. So instead of closing its doors, the little congregation opened them—free of charge. Soon their building became a hub of activity, with an after-school program, AA meetings, and exercise groups.

The happy postscript to this story is that some of the neighbors began to show up for worship on Sunday mornings. Over time, the struggling congregation became a thriving community of faith that is much more diverse than it had been before, and that continues to serve its neighbors—whether there is anything "in it" for the congregation or not.

That last bit is important. When we "give ourselves away" according to Jesus' command, we can't be sure there is anything in it for us. We may well end up without a coat *or* a shirt! (In much the same way, Julio Diaz could have ended up losing his life as well as his wallet!) Jesus' command to do unto others as we would have them do to us has no conditions, no fine print that somehow allows us to see first to our own self-interest. It's simple, even though it's not easy: *Just do it.*

What would the world look like if the Christian community gave itself away like this—no strings attached? It's hard to know. But we can be sure that in the process we would "give away" something central to the good news of Jesus Christ . . . and it would be a powerful witness.

## Think It Over

1. Why is it so hard to do as Jesus says in these verses?

2. What would it mean for your congregation to "lose its shirt" in your community?

## In Other Words

"When a Christian meets with injustice, he no longer clings to his rights and defends them at all costs. He is absolutely free from possessions and bound to Christ alone."

—Dietrich Bonhoeffer, *The Cost of Discipleship*

## Live It Out

Volunteer some of your time in a community outreach program. If your congregation doesn't have any—start some!

# The Pursuit of Justice 3

*"When you spread out your hands in prayer, I will hide my eyes from you; even if you offer many prayers, I will not listen. Your hands are full of blood; wash and make yourselves clean.*
*Take your evil deeds out of my sight!*
*Stop doing wrong, learn to do right! Seek justice, encourage the oppressed. Defend the cause of the fatherless, plead the case of the widow."*
—Isaiah 1:15-17

How would you feel? How would you feel if someone came up to greet you and extended a hand that was covered with blood?

Most of us would recoil in horror—and that's pretty much God's reaction in the first chapter of Isaiah as well. God refuses to listen to the people's prayers because their "hands are full of blood" (Isa. 1:15). It's not that God does not want their worship; it's that God doesn't want worship from those who refuse to walk their talk.

It's tempting to read passages like this and assume they are about somebody else. But are they really?

Once I attended a denominational meeting where we received a carefully considered recommendation asking us as a community of faith to speak out in protest against the United States government's use of torture. Many thoughtful people came to the microphone to argue against the recommendation on the grounds that national security demands the use of "coercive tactics." Extraordinary circumstances, they argued, called for extraordinary measures. In the end, we voted not to speak out.

Is there blood on our hands?

Part of the problem in such discussions is the idea that faith and politics don't mix. Yet, if Christian communities of faith do not speak out in the midst of civil society, how will the gospel be heard? How can we expect to bear witness in that society when we do not have the courage of our own convictions? And as the Isaiah passage points out, how can we expect God to have any regard for our prayers? We may be able to convince ourselves, but God is not so easily fooled.

Both the possibilities and the challenges of such witnessing are illustrated in the tale of one congregation's experience.

When a large Baptist congregation with considerable resources heard that an elderly Polish-American Catholic woman in their town was about to lose her home to a predatory mortgage company, they stepped in. First they bought the woman's house; then they allowed her to make reasonable payments on a low-interest loan so that she could eventually own her home.

The media was all over the story—lauding the congregation for its generosity and its willingness to "put their money where their mouth is." But the congregation got a much cooler reception when they approached government representatives about taking steps to end the predatory loan practices that had led to the problem in the first place.

The pastor of that church commented that the powers that be don't mind when the church does "churchy" things. But the minute the church moves from the priestly to the prophetic—look out!

Sometimes resistance to seeking justice comes from within—as in the example of the denomination's refusal to protest torture. Sometimes it comes from without— as in the example of the congregation trying to combat unfair lending practices. But the important thing to remember is that seeking justice is not an optional activity for Christian communities. It is part of our gospel DNA.

> **Word Alert**
>
> The Hebrew word for *justice* is *mishpat*. It carries connotations of "right" and "rectitude." Proverbs 21:15 says that justice "brings joy to the righteous."

Perhaps part of the problem for Reformed Christians is that we have put so much emphasis on being saved *by grace through faith*. Surely part of our grateful response to this gift should involve the passionate pursuit of justice!

Fortunately those of us who are part of the Christian community know how to "get clean" once we have "come clean." If there is blood on our hands, we know the One who can wash them clean. And once our hands have been washed clean, we can bear powerful, grateful witness by seeking justice, loving kindness, and walking humbly with our God (Mic. 6:8).

## Think It Over

1. How does our tendency toward individualism make it harder to see the blood on our hands as a Christian community?

2. What's staining your Christian community's hands? (Think locally, nationally, and globally.)

## In Other Words

"Your stand for justice and right, your witness, your prayers and your caring and concern are what change the planet—these things do not just evaporate and disappear."

—Archbishop Desmond Tutu, *God Has a Dream*

## Live It Out

Do at least one thing today that would make the prophet Isaiah proud.

# Tear Down These Walls! 4

*"In Christ Jesus you are all children of God through faith, for all of you who were baptized into Christ have clothed yourselves with Christ. There is neither Jew nor Gentile, neither slave nor free, neither male nor female, for you are all one in Christ Jesus."*

—Galatians 3:26-28

The book of Galatians is sometimes called the "Magna Carta of Christian liberty." In it, Paul systematically demolishes the arguments that were propping up the dividing walls in the Christian community at Galatia. One of the biggest walls had been erected by those who said you had to become a Jew before you became a Christian. Even though Paul himself had come to Christ as a devout Jew, he argues in Galatians that faith is the only real requirement for becoming a Christian (2:15-21).

But there were other walls in the Galatian church too, and it's as if Paul can't stop knocking them down once he gets started. By the time he gets to chapter 3 he's kicking down all the divisions: not just the wall between

## Word Alert

The *Magna Carta* was a charter passed in England in 1215 that guaranteed certain basic liberties. Even today it is recognized as a watershed document; it often lends its name to other documents that support basic rights and privileges.

Jews and Greeks but those between slaves and free people and male and female.

Pretty radical stuff! Imagine the buzz that must have gone around the first-century congregation as they listened to Paul's letter being read. Slaves must have stolen surprised glances at their masters; husbands and wives must have been afraid to look at each other at all! No doubt Paul's letter provoked many intense conversations in the church parking lot that day.

Some of Paul's words still strike us as radical today. We are, after all, still working on what it means that in our community "there is no longer male and female." But other divisions plague us as well, and Paul's logic applies to them too. If we are "one in Christ Jesus," why are there still walls of race, tribe, and class within the Christian community?

It's often said that Sunday morning between 11 and 12:00 is the most segregated hour of the week. What does that say about our witness?

Christians in the Evangelical Covenant Church have decided to tackle the racial divide in an intense and creative way. One of their efforts involves four-day bus trips through the American South that highlight "how far we have come, and how far we have to go." The journey is as much about attitude as it is about miles. It is described as "an intentional, cross-racial prayer journey" that "seeks to assist disciples of Christ as they move toward a righteous response to the social ills related to racism."

This positive step must gladden God's heart. But there are so many other examples that must grieve God's heart. One of the most tragic examples of our failure to live out our unity in Christ comes from within the Reformed family of churches.

Reformed Church in America General Secretary Wes Granberg-Michaelson calls our attention to a situation in Kenya where division turned deadly. In Kenya's Rift Valley, Reformed Christians began killing each other in the aftermath of Kenya's contested presidential election. It seems that the Christians of the Presbyterian Church of East Africa and those of the Reformed Church of Kenya are largely made up of two different tribes—each backing a different presidential candidate. When the election became contested, "tribal loyalties [erased] Christian identity" (*The Church Herald*, April 2008). At least 1,500 people died, and as many as 300,000 were displaced. Granberg-Michaelson concludes:

> The task of healing and reconciliation at the local level . . . begins with a deeper understanding of Christian discipleship, affirming that allegiance to Jesus Christ is at the heart of our identity and transcends racial, ethnic, tribal, cultural, and national claims of loyalty.

The Belhar Confession (1986) is one resource that comes to Christians everywhere as a gift from the church in South Africa. According to one member of the Uniting Reformed Church of Southern Africa (URCSA), "We carry this confession on behalf of all the Reformed churches. We do not think of it as ours alone."

> We believe that unity is . . . both a gift and an obligation for the church of Jesus Christ; that through the working of God's Spirit it is a binding force, yet simultaneously a reality which must be earnestly pursued and sought: one which the people of God must continually be built up to attain (Eph. 4:1-16).
> —*Confession of Belhar*

**Web Alert**

To read the entire Belhar Confession online, visit www.rca.org and type Belhar Confession in the search box.

The Belhar is one of the tools we can use to help demolish the walls that divide us and impair our witness to the world.

## Think It Over

1. What are the dividing walls in your community of faith?

2. What are you doing about them?

## In Other Words

"The endless divisions that we create between us and that we live and die for—whether they are our religions, our ethnic groups, our nationalities—are so totally irrelevant to God."

—Archbishop Desmond Tutu, *God Has a Dream*

## Live It Out

Take down one brick in a wall that exists in your congregation: make a phone call, write a letter, or initiate a conversation that begins to tear down this wall!

# Care for Creation 5

> *"The creation waits in eager expectation for the children of God to be revealed. For the creation was subjected to frustration, not by its own choice, but by the will of the one who subjected it, in hope that the creation itself will be liberated from its bondage to decay and brought into the freedom and glory of the children of God. We know that the whole creation has been groaning as in the pains of childbirth right up to the present time. Not only so, but we ourselves . . ."*
>
> **—Romans 8:19-23a**

A poem written by Laurence Houseman in 1919 asks this pointed question: "How shall we love thee, holy, hidden Being, if we love not the world which thou has made?"

How shall we, indeed?

Houseman's poem (set to music by Geoffrey Shaw in the hymn "Father Eternal, Ruler of Creation") is amazingly "modern" in its concern for creation. For whatever reason, Christians have been among the last to catch on to the fact that we have a responsibility to care for God's creation, and that this responsibility is directly connected to our faith.

One person who has led the faith community in this area is Calvin DeWitt, professor of environmental studies at the University of Wisconsin-Madison and—among other things—cofounder of the International Evangelical Environmental Network. To fully appreciate the effect that DeWitt has had on the evangelical community in this regard, imagine the action of turning a sleeve right-side out. It's as if the Holy Spirit reached in and grasped DeWitt, pulling the whole evangelical Christian community along after him.

On the back of his book *Earth-Wise: A Biblical Response to Environmental Issues*, DeWitt expresses his hope that the first thing the church will do is to "regain a joyful, positive attitude about our ability to work for good in the world." Ours, he says,

> is not to grovel in polluted gutters or to wring our hands over our sins. Instead, we are called to go about reclaiming creation for our Lord, knowing that "the earth is the Lord's and everything in it" (Ps 24:1).

DeWitt's words point us to Scripture's clear and consistent call to be caretakers of creation. In Genesis 2, God puts our first parents in the garden to "till it and to keep it" (v. 15). And since the word for "keep" also means to "watch over," we get a clear sense of what God intended. When Paul talks about the whole creation "groaning in labor pains" as it awaits the day when it (and we!) are set free from our "bondage to decay," he speaks out of the conviction that God's ultimate plan involves the renewal of creation.

That's a plan all of us in the Christian community are called to be a part of.

When Christians work together to preserve and restore the environment, we are bearing witness to God's love for creation and God's plan to renew all creation in and through Jesus Christ.

So why has it taken us so long to get this? I wonder if it's partly because we have been so preoccupied with "saving souls."

N. T. Wright begins a chapter ("New Creation, Starting Now") of his book *Simply Christian* with this shocking statement: "Despite what many people think . . . the point of Christianity isn't 'to go to heaven when you die.'"

What *is* the point then? we ask, scratching our heads.

It turns out God has much more in mind. As Wright puts it:

> The New Testament picks up from the Old the theme that God intends, in the end, to put the whole creation to rights. Earth and heaven were made to overlap with one another, not fitfully, mysteriously, and partially as they do at the moment, but completely, gloriously, and utterly.

God's plan, says Wright, is not to abandon this world but to remake it. And when he does, he will raise all his people to new bodily life to live in it. That is the promise of the Christian gospel.

And that is something we as the Christian community can bear witness to!

## Think It Over

1. What place does repentance play in our witness on this issue of creation care?

2. How could the Holy Spirit used you as the "cuff" to turn your whole faith community right-side out?

## In Other Words

"This is my Father's world; O let us not forget
that though the wrong is great and strong, God is the ruler yet.
He trusts us with his world, to keep it clean and fair—
all earth and trees, all skies and seas,
all creatures everywhere."

—Maltbie Davenport Babcock, 1901; rev. Mary Babcock Crawford, 1972

## Live It Out

Start a recycling program in your church. If you already have one,
praise God and get the word out!

# Session 5
# Witness
## Discussion Guide

With all the challenges we've discussed, let's remember that Christian community is still Exhibit A of God's gospel message to the world. Jesus told his disciples, "By this everyone will know that you are my disciples, if you love one another" (John 13:35). And the early church father Tertullian wrote of the church's persecutors: "But it is mainly the deeds of a love so noble that lead many to put a brand upon us. See, they say, how they love one another . . . how they are ready even to die for one another. . . ."

The Christian community is more than a gathering place, more than an incubator of faith and love. It is a witness to the world of God's love and salvation. When we live in love, stand up for justice, testify to the truth, and act with deeds of mercy, we become Exhibit A before the jury of public opinion.

## Welcome and Prayer
*(5 minutes—give or take)*

Part of the point of meeting together is to allow the Holy Spirit to form us into a community of faith and learning. **Invite God's blessing** on this group of disciples with the following prayer:

**God of all creation, you have set us in this world to do your will. As we gather today around your Word, shine in our hearts, our minds, and our hands so that we may learn more about what it means to let your light shine to all the world; through Jesus Christ our Lord, Amen.**

## Option

Have a volunteer open the session with a brief prayer along the lines of the one suggested above.

## For Starters
*(10 minutes)*

**Welcome everyone back to the group.** Remind participants that the theme for the week is the witness of the Christian community, and **invite everyone to share one thing about this congregation's witness that attracted them.**

Or invite group members to share one insight from the daily devotions that was meaningful for them. Don't discuss it now, just mention it.

## Let's Focus
*(2 minutes)*

**Reflect silently** on the following statement:

**The church does not exist for itself, but as a witness to the reign of God in all of life and as the firstfruit of the kingdom of God.**

Then have someone **read the statement aloud in segments,** allowing a space for reflection in between each phrase:

**The church does not exist for itself
but as a witness to the reign of God
in all of life
and as the firstfruit of the kingdom of God.**

## Word Search
*(20 minutes)*

**Read one or more of the following Scripture passages aloud and discuss the questions that follow (or others of your own).**

- Isaiah 42:5-7

  In this passage, one of the "Servant Songs" from Isaiah, the prophet points to the coming Messiah, but also describes the community of God's people, Israel, and the church. In what specific ways are God's people called to be a "light to the gentiles?"

  What would that look like in your church?

- Matthew 5:13-16

  What are some ways in which the church is the "salt of the earth?"

  In what specific way does Jesus tell us to be a "light to the world?"

  Why do you think he calls for "good deeds" and not good words?

- 1 Peter 2:9-10

  What do you think Peter means here that the church is a "chosen people . . . God's special possession"?

  What is the relationship between our chosenness (election) and our witness to the world?

  How do we sometimes misunderstand election?

# Bring It Home
*(20 minutes)*

**Choose one of the following options.**

## Option 1

Using newsprint or a board, **make a list together of all the activities and ministries of your congregation.** After you have completed the list, discuss to what extent your church "does not exist for itself but as a witness to the reign of God." Given the gifts and talents of the members and the location of your congregation, what ministries might be added to increase this witness?

## Option 2

**As time permits, choose from among the following questions and discuss them:**

• The "Let's Focus" statement says, "The church does not exist for itself." What are some of the ways the church tends to exist for itself? Does this sometimes happen in your church? If so, what can be done to change this?

• Discuss some of the ways in which the Christian community in North America has been a "witness to the reign of God" and some of the ways it has not.

• As Reformed Christians we believe that Christ claims all of life for his kingdom. What areas of life in North America today do you think do you think especially need the witness of the church? Might this endanger the church's spiritual message?

## Option 3

Hand out copies of your church's hymnal or songbook. **Browse through the index to find hymns about our witness. Choose one or two of them to sing or read together, and then discuss what insights they have about our everyday witness as disciples.**

# Pray It Through
*(10 minutes)*

**Invite participants to raise concerns and/or thanksgivings** they would like to include in the group's prayer. Especially remember to pray for your church to be a witness to God's kingdom in its life and ministry. As items are raised, you may wish to write them on slips of paper and "gift" them to someone else in the group who is willing to voice that particular request during the group's prayer. Keep in mind that it is a powerful thing to hear others voice the prayers that are on our hearts. This is one of the most beautiful embodiments of Christian community.

You may choose to simply **ask one person to open and close the prayer, with others using the slips of paper to prompt the prayers in between.** Remember that it is fine to simply read the request and then leave a short period of silence for all to unite silently in prayer around each item.

**The following "template" may be used for the prayer as well:**

Heavenly Father, thank you for this time together. As you have gathered us here today, so gather now our prayers for each other, our communities, and the world.

*As each request/thanksgiving is read, leave a short period of silence for all to unite silently in prayer around that item. After each period of silence, punctuate the prayer with the following:*

**Leader:** Lord, in your mercy

**People:** hear our prayer.

If your group enjoys singing, you may wish to end this final session of *Living in Community* by praying or singing "Song of Hope" (*Sing! A New Creation,* 282) in Spanish and English.

## Live It Out
*(All next week)*

Look for one thing each day that you can do to strengthen the witness of your congregation. Partner with someone else from the group so that you can check in and hold each other up in prayer.

> **Web Alert**
>
> **Be sure to check out the participants' section for this session on www.GrowDisciples.org for interesting links and suggestions for readings and other activities that will deepen your understanding of living in community.**